S0-AKH-571

VIOLETTE SZABO

by the same author

Dambuster – A Life of Guy Gibson VC (Leo Cooper, 1994)
She Who Dared (with Jackie George) (Leo Cooper, 1999)

VIOLETTE SZABO

The Life That I Have

by

Susan Ottaway

LEO COOPER

First published in Great Britain in 2002 by
LEO COOPER
an imprint of Pen & Sword Books
47 Church Street
Barnsley
South Yorkshire
S70 2AS

ISBN 085052 780 5

A catalogue record for this book
is available from the British Library

Typeset in 11/13pt Sabon by
Phoenix Typesetting, Ilkley, West Yorkshire

Printed by CPI UK.

For Sharon, Laurie, Lizzy and Lorna

Contents

Foreword

When Susan Ottaway invited me to write a brief introduction to her biography of Violette Szabo I was surprised because I never met Violette, although I was well aware of her progress, eagerness and determination as she passed through the paramilitary training course at the Special Training School at Inverie, an isolated shooting lodge in Knoydart, accessible only by sea voyage from the fishing port of Mallaig at the western tip of Lochaber in Scotland.

I realized it was a real privilege to receive such an invitation, for Violette Szabo was one of the great heroines among those women who served the Special Operations Executive on dangerous missions in enemy-occupied territory, and she was one of the thirteen who died by the hands of the Nazis in their German Concentration Camps.

The Specials Operations Executive, previously known as SO 2, was officially set up in July 1940 to train volunteers of various nationalities for clandestine operations in all enemy-occupied territories in Europe, and to organize resistance groups against the Nazi invaders. To provide training on the scale envisaged, the new organization had to have various types of schools in different parts of the UK. Already it had certain properties in England, and some of them were set aside as Preliminary Schools where volunteers could be given initial screening, undergoing a certain amount of elementary training during a probationary period, when unsuitable or undesirable types could be dismissed. It was decided that paramilitary training would be carried out in the West Highlands of Scotland which had been declared No. 1 protected area, entry to which was at all points of access controlled and an official entry pass was required. Residents living within the area were obliged to apply for a Resident's Pass to allow exit and re-entry.

In due course ten lodges and large houses were requisitioned in the countryside around Arisaig, with Arisaig House as the HQ of the group, which was named Group A. The nature of the terrain, with its hills and glens and undulating heathery moors, was such that all the ten houses were screened from one another and activities carried on at each of them could not be observed or overlooked; security and safety were ideally available.

In 1942 I was appointed SLO STS (Scotland), Security Liaison Officer Special Training Schools Scotland, with responsibility for the safety and security of all STS in Scotland, which had hitherto been provided by the 49 F.S. Section in Fort William, but SOE had decided it should itself be responsible for its own security in the Scottish Schools.

Because of the scattered nature of the Group A schools I had security NCOs stationed at various places who reported directly to me each week, keeping me informed as to which Country Section teams were under training and anything else that was going on, and I myself made routine visits to check and to discuss any problems that might arise with the individual commandants. So it was that I became aware of the team in which Violette Szabo played an important part.

The paramilitary course was at first limited to three weeks but this was soon found to be too short a time to cover the full syllabus, and it was extended to five weeks, which became the norm, except for special circumstances. It was intended to be a physically demanding training and it certainly was. It covered a wide range of subjects including physical training, much tougher than the normal Army PT, out of doors in all weathers, and that included preparatory exercises for parachuting; weapons training, particularly in small arms and hand guns, such as the .32 or .45 pistol; demolition training and the safe handling of explosives; map reading and compass work; fieldcraft over open country; 'Silent Killing' – an advanced form of unarmed combat and much more dangerous, which could be practised only on life-sized dummies. There was no distinction between the sexes; to their instructors they were all just 'bods in battledress' and they all went through the same wet crawling over boggy moors and hills; all suffered the same soakings, the tired muscles and aching joints at the end of each day.

Country Sections made up teams of about six men and/or women from those who had successfully passed the Preliminary Schools' screening, and they were sent to Group A for the toughening-up process. After the course at Group A they went for parachute training to Ringway, near Manchester. From there they went to the Finishing Schools in the New Forest area, known collectively as Group B, where they were given instruction in security, secret service methods and in propaganda. At no point during their training was the word 'agent' ever mentioned, but by the time they reached Group B most of the trainees had a good idea of what was expected of them. Each team was small in number which gave their instructors and trainers the opportunity to keep almost individual watch over each of them, and the Security NCO also sent individual reports to his Section Head.

It was during her training at Ringway that Violette Szabo made an unsafe landing from one of her parachute jumps, injuring her ankle very badly, and it was that same ankle that, later on, led to her capture in the field.

The immense amount of research that Susan Ottaway has put into the compiling of this biography reveals not only the strong determination of Violette to avenge the death of her husband at El Alamein and the remarkable bravery she displayed in France in the normal day-to-day dangerous atmosphere in which she worked, but also the huge reserve of courage she showed in the hands of the Gestapo and in the concentration camp of Ravensbrück, where she was shot on 25 January 1945.

I must express sincere thanks to Susan Ottaway for bringing to public attention the story of one of our great heroines of those war years, in whose memory there is now a Memorial Museum at Wormelow, near Hereford.

'Aonghais' Adamson Fyffe.
Scotland, September 2001.

Acknowledgements

When I approached Pen & Sword Books about the possibility of writing a book about Violette Szabo, Henry Wilson, the Publishing Manager, agreed to a contract provided I managed to speak to Violette's daughter, Tania, and obtain her cooperation. I was very nervous about meeting her, but we got along extremely well. We talked for many hours and she fetched out boxes of information she had collected over the years about her mother. Many more hours were spent going through the contents and reading letters sent to her both by people who admired Violette and by people who actually knew her. Tania is a lovely person and we have remained in touch. I truly value her friendship.

Roy Bushell, Violette's brother, has been wonderful. He has answered my questions with patience and good humour and has provided many of the family details that I have been able to include in the book. Likewise Norman Lucas, Violette's cousin, has been very helpful.

In the initial stages of my research I remembered that I had worked with a girl, Val Weir, whose uncle had corresponded with Violette Szabo's father. I remembered how she had borrowed from her uncle a powder compact that had belonged to Violette and had been given to him by Violette's parents, Charles and Reine Bushell, and had brought it into the office to show me. Mr and Mrs Bushell said that it had been a wedding present, but I now believe that it may have been a gift from Maurice Buckmaster, before Violette's first mission to France. It still had a trace of the face powder that Violette had used in it. I knew that

Val's uncle had since died and I had not been in touch with Val herself for some years. On the off chance that she might have some of her uncle's papers, I telephoned her. She told me that her uncle's wife had died two days before my call and that her house was being cleared as we spoke. She thought it unlikely that any papers had survived, but promised to call me if there was anything that might be useful for my book. Some days later I received a call from her that sent goose pimples down my spine. She had just returned from her aunt's funeral. After the service her will had been read and in it she left what she called 'The Violette Szabo Collection' to my friend Val. Val promised that as soon as she had gone through it all she would let me have a look. True to her word she not only let me look, she lent me the entire collection to keep for as long as I needed it. I owe Val a huge debt of gratitude.

I was privileged to be able to speak to some of the leading figures in SOE and related organizations, including the late Vera Atkins, Yvonne Baseden, Jean Claude Guiet, Bob Maloubier, the late Leo Marks and 'Hélène', who worked with the Resistance, was captured and met up again with Violette Szabo while they were both imprisoned in Ravensbrück concentration camp. She didn't want to be named, but she has my grateful thanks for the trouble she took in telling me her very moving story.

Thanks also to Duncan Stuart, SOE Advisor at the Foreign & Commonwealth Office, for his endless patience in dealing with my huge amount of queries, and to Valerie Collins, also of the Foreign & Commonwealth office for her thoughtfulness and for the beautifully presented information.

Without the help of librarian Audrey Ford my task would have been impossible. Audrey has been a constant source of both information and support and I am so grateful to her for everything she has done on my behalf.

Thanks to Aonghais Fyffe for his splendid description of the training at Arisaig, for numerous other facts, and for agreeing to write the foreword to this book.

Thanks are also due to Stephan Barton for the information about the camp at Saarbrücken and for the photo; to Steve Gowler and his daughter, Stephanie, of Berea, Kentucky, for sending me the photo of the execution alley at Ravensbrück; to

Colonel Pierre-Richard Kohn of the French Embassy and Colonel Hans-Werner Fritz of the German Embassy, both in London; to Kapitänleutnant M.A. Arold of the Militärgeschichtliches Forschungsamt in Potsdam, Germany; to Denise Delmas and Françoise Legrand, both of the Levallois-Perret archives; the staff in the office of the Mairie de Levallois-Perret in France; to Paul McCue for the trouble he has taken to provide me with many beautiful photos; to John Wilkinson for the book cover; to editor Tom Hartman; to Henry Wilson at Pen & Sword Books and to Barbara Bramall, Production Manager at Pen & Sword, for all her hard work on my behalf and for her support and good humour; to my niece, Laurie Davidson, for her translations, and to the following people, all of whom have made valuable contributions:

Susan Andrews, Bett Bailey, Gary Baines, Janet Bastin, Peter Bond, Brian Bunyard, Juanita Carberry, Thomas Chapman, Keith Cook, Stephen Cox, Cyril Cunningham, Barbara and Marcus Davidson, Marianna Disalle, Phillipa Dolley, the late David Earle, Craig Evans, Michael Flynn, Liana del Giudice, Carolyn Hammond, Valerie Hansford, Mrs Harris, David Harrison, Stephen Harwood, John Haslett, Tony Hawkins, Keith Hayward, Mr Heath, Ian Howard, Eileen Hughes, Rhian James, Lucy Jones, Miss H. Jude, Herr Kalle, Paul Kendall, Mr and Mrs P. Kolind, Paul Lacey, Mrs Lambert, Bob Large, Gordon Leith, Peter Hope Lumley, Dave Lunn, Richard Marshall, Phil Martin, Terence Mason, Sidney Mathews, Elizabeth McCrum, John Melbourne, Linda Morgan, Ben Nock, Gordon Nornable, Bob Oram, Jean Overton Fuller, Clive Peerless, Andrew Perry, Lieutenant Colonel John Pitt, Ron Phillips, Bernadette Quinn, Laura Redwood, Anthony Richards, Rosemary Rigby, Dorothy and Jack Ringlesbach, Mr V. Robinson, Alison Roper, Susie Rowe, Mr W. Rudd, Ian and Ray Rushton, Margaret Scott, Carl Sheridan, Roger Sims, David South, Lee Speakman, Al Terwiliger, Wendy Thirkettle, Steve Tomlinson, Alison Townsend, Philip Vickers, David Walker, Stephen Walton, Tara Wenger and Sue Williamson.

If there are any others whose names I have omitted, I offer my apologies and my thanks.

* * *

My final thanks go to my partner Nick who, as always, has been a tower of strength, has given me constant help and encouragement, has fixed the computer when I've broken it and has done more than his fair share of the housework while I've been lost in my own little world of research and writing. Thanks, Nick, you're brilliant!

Susan Ottaway
Summer 2001.

Introduction

Violette Szabo was my childhood heroine. She was everything I aspired to be – beautiful, clever and brave. Her example inspired me to study French and German so that I would be ready, should the need ever arise again, to do the sort of work that she had done. It did not take me very long to discover that I was not, and never would be, SOE material. Although language was important, the qualities required of an SOE agent were so much more than the mere ability to speak French.

My first book was about Wing Commander Guy Gibson VC, leader of the famous Dambuster raid in 1943, who had also been one of my heroes when I was a child. I would have loved to write a book about Violette Szabo as well, but *Carve Her Name With Pride* by R.J. Minney had been published many years before and was a great success. I thought that I had missed my chance.

Then, one morning in October 1998, I heard a piece about Violette Szabo on the Radio 4 programme, *Woman's Hour*. I had been told that the market could take one new biography about the same person every ten years but I was doubtful if that were really true. However, I realized that it had been forty-two years since the publication of *Carve Her Name With Pride,* and the fact that there were still programmes on national radio about her, fifty-three years after her death, seemed to prove that there was still an interest in this brave young woman.

People saw her in so many different ways. I could not even get any agreement from those who knew her about the way she spoke. Her accent was described as being French, Cockney, like a

Londoner and even like mine, which I suppose could be described as standard southern English.

I was surprised by the reactions I had to my requests for help while I was researching Violette's story. Some people promised much and delivered very little, in some cases nothing at all. The people of whom I expected little often gave a great deal. I have been shown an enormous amount of kindness from people all over the world, from Australia and USA, to France, Germany and Great Britain.

There does seem to be a little group of people who regard Violette Szabo as their personal property and are unwilling to impart to others any information at all. I came to the conclusion that many of this group had very little information to give. The book and the film, *Carve Her Name With Pride*, have both shown her as being an almost perfect being and the little band of her supporters still describe her in superlatives; even Odette Hallowes called her 'the bravest of us all'. Perhaps they are frightened that another book about their idol might destroy the myth. Perhaps it will. The woman that I discovered in my research was much less perfect than she had been portrayed, but certainly much more interesting and real.

She has been described as being fearless. She was certainly a daredevil who would attempt things that others would not, but does that make her fearless? I have always thought that fearless people lack the wit and imagination to appreciate the dangers they are facing. Truly courageous people know the dangers but press on regardless of their personal well-being. I like to think that Violette Szabo falls into that latter category.

It soon became obvious to me that it would be impossible to write about her without including in some detail the people with whom she lived, worked and died. They were all brave people of whom very little has been written in the years since the Second World War. When people hear the name Violette Szabo, most of them recognize it, but how many people know very much about Denise Bloch or Lilian Rolfe or, for that matter, the others, men and women, who went to France and to other countries in occupied Europe and beyond, and fought just as bravely? They, along with many, many other young people, died for the sake of our freedom and they deserve some recognition. So, too, do those who did not die but continued their fight in difficult conditions, often being arrested and sent to survive as best they could in the ghastly concentration camps of Europe.

I had hoped that I would find the answers to all my questions about Violette and, to a certain extent, I have. But my search for answers has also thrown up many more questions and puzzles; it has been a fascinating journey.

Chapter One

Childhood

George Bushell was the landlord of the White Hart public house in Church Street, in the little Berkshire village of Hampstead Norreys, north-east of Newbury, famous for its racecourse. Soon after the birth of their third daughter, George's wife died, leaving him with three young children to bring up, as well as a public house to run. Within a year George had remarried and he and his second wife, Elizabeth, had a son, Charles, to be followed, some years later, by a daughter, Florence Constance.

George and Elizabeth worked hard running the pub and George supplemented his income by game-keeping and manufacturing 'whiting'. There was a pit behind the pub from which he obtained the chalk for the whiting. This was then dried and ground up to make a smooth powder, which was used as a cleaning substance or for the manufacture of whitewash. The River Pang, which bordered the grounds of the pub, provided fish for both food and sport and the Bushells took in bed-and-breakfast guests at the pub, who came mainly for the fishing. The White Hart was, and still is, a pretty building, with a pool in the back garden in which the children could swim. George had made it by digging out a part of the river bank and slightly diverting the course of the river. It was a lovely place in which to grow up and Charles and Florence shared a happy childhood with their half-sisters, Sarah, Katherine and Clara, who were, for some unexplained reason, always called by their second names, Annie, Dora and Mabel. Although during the time that George was landlord at the White Hart, it was a happy family home, it had not always been so. At least three of its former landlords had ended their days in the local asylum.

As he grew up, George and Elizabeth's only son took up poaching and soon gained quite a reputation in the area, being pursued on several occasions by the village policeman. In later years, when visiting his family from his home in London, he would often seek out another poacher, known in the village as 'Miggy Whirl', and do a deal with him, returning home with a box of poached birds, rabbits and fish which he would sell to local grocers' shops. Although he had a number of different jobs and found it hard to settle in one place for long periods of time, he was, in fact, a hard worker. He was always on the lookout for new ways of providing for his family, even if his methods were sometimes rather unorthodox. His nephew, Norman Lucas, remembers Charles, or Charlie as he was more usually known, as being a 'loveable rogue'. Norman's own father, Harry Lucas, was also a publican. He was the landlord at the New Inn, which was also in Hampstead Norreys, about a quarter of a mile down the hill from the White Hart.

At the start of the First World War Charles joined the army and became a driver with the Royal Army Service Corps. He was posted to France where he met a pretty young French girl called Reine Blanche Leroy. She was the daughter of a notary clerk living in Quevauvillers, a small town south-west of Amiens, in the département of the Somme. Reine had been born in Quevauvillers but the family had originally come from Pont Rémy, on the River Somme, south-east of Abbeville. Her mother had died at an early age and she had become very close to her father's sisters, her aunts Blanche and Berthe, and to her own sister, Marguerite.

Charles and Reine married in Pont Rémy after a courtship which started in the dark days of the Battle of the Somme and continued until 1918. It could hardly have been called a whirlwind romance as the wedding took place over two years after they first met. They began their married life by coming to England at the end of the war and settled in Hampstead Norreys with Charles's family at the White Hart.

In 1920 their first child, a son, arrived and was named Roy. He was born in Wandsworth, but his birth certificate shows his mother's address as the White Hart in Hampstead Norreys and he has no idea why his mother was in Wandsworth at the time of his birth.

The family stayed in England for a very short time before returning to France. They found an apartment in the town of Levallois-Perret to the north-west of Paris, in the département of Hauts-de-Seine. It was, and still is, a pleasant little town, busy and bustling during the week and sleepy at the weekends. It was here, at 72 rue de Villiers, that Charles and Reine's second child, a daughter they named Violette Reine Elizabeth, was born at six a.m. on 26 June 1921. It has been said that she was born at the British hospital in Paris. This hospital, now called the Hôpital Franco Britannique, is located in Levallois-Perret; indeed the older part of the hospital is in rue de Villiers, but at number 48 not 72. Sadly Violette's birthplace no longer exists. It has been replaced by a modern office block but the staff at the Hôpital Franco Britannique assured me that 72 rue de Villiers was never part of the hospital. So it would seem that Violette was born at home.

For a time it looked as if the growing family might stay permanently in France. Work was scarce in England and Charles decided to buy a car and run a private hire service in Paris. Reine supplemented their income with dressmaking, which had been her profession before her marriage. She spent at lot of her time at home with her two children as her husband was often away overnight and sometimes for days at a time, ferrying his clients all over France. Reine would have been happy to remain in her homeland but things were becoming increasingly difficult economically. The employment options open to Charles were rather limited as he had never been able to master the French language. He and Reine discussed what to do and came to the conclusion that they would be better off returning to England to stay with Charles's family. So, when Violette was about three years old, they packed their bags again, gave up their small flat and moved back to rural Berkshire.

When George Bushell gave up the tenancy of the White Hart he took over the running of a shop in Station Yard in Hampstead Norreys. In the early 1920s he also decided to start a small bus company and went into partnership with a local man called 'Batty' Wheeler, running a bus between the village and Newbury.

It was later absorbed into the Newbury & District Bus Company. On his return to England Charles went to work for his father, driving the bus. There were a number of small bus companies at that time, all competing with each other for business. In Hampstead Norreys alone there were five other companies, Fulker & Son, Jeffrey, Johnson, Matthews and W.J. White & Son, as well as George Bushell and his son, all plying the route to Newbury and stopping to pick up passengers along the way. It was a precarious business and life was difficult for the Bushell family. Although Roy remembers living for a time at the White Hart, he has much stronger memories of living with his father's sister, Aunt Dora, and of being sent to a convent, although he cannot recall where it was.

By the mid-1920s Roy and Violette once again left England. Their parents took them to France where Roy went to Quevauvillers to live with his great-aunt, Tante Blanche, and Violette to Noyelles-sur-Somme where she stayed with Tante Marguerite. Charles and Reine Bushell then returned to England where, for a time, Charles became a used car dealer. Roy and Violette were not to see very much of either of their parents or of each other for several years, until in 1932 both children returned to England. By then their parents were living in Talbot Road in Bayswater and Roy and Violette had two more brothers, John and Noel.

They soon moved to the Stockwell–Brixton borders of south London where they rented rooms from a woman called Mrs Tripp at 12 Stockwell Park Walk, just behind the Astoria cinema. The road itself still exists; it is a small, busy, one-way street linking Stockwell Road to Brixton Road. The house in which they lived was the first of four large Victorian dwellings on the left-hand side as you turned in from Stockwell Road, just around the corner from the Brixton Tabernacle. The house has long gone, having been replaced by a row of modern houses. In the 1930s, however, Stockwell Park Walk was home to many theatrical people and was a lively, interesting place.

Charles Bushell had still not settled in one job at this time, although he was always looking for the one that would provide him with long-term security. The burden of being the breadwinner fell mainly to Reine, who was an excellent dressmaker. Eileen

Hughes, who was a neighbour in Stockwell Park Walk, remembered Mrs Bushell as being rather dour and serious, possibly the result of the strain of providing for her growing family. Mr Bushell, on the other hand, was cheerful and smiling and often spoke in a kindly way to the neighbourhood children. This seems to have been rather at odds with the way he behaved at home. Roy has described him as,

> 'very strict; a martinet, in fact. It was only Mother's restraining influence that kept some semblance of domestic bliss in our household. At the time we were not overly fond of him, but to be fair he was a pretty good father, and we were well cared for.'

Although Violette was older than Eileen, the two girls would sometimes play hopscotch together on the pavements of Stockwell Park Walk and could be seen hanging out of their respective windows in the evenings, having a chat. Eileen remembered the Bushell boys as often playing childish pranks like trying to tie tin cans to cats' tails. They were lively, boisterous children and Violette was no different from her brothers. She was always active and full of energy. The Bushell children often spoke in French among themselves, which annoyed some of the neighbours who assumed they were being talked about.

As well as playing with Eileen, Violette became friendly with Mrs Tripp's niece, Winnie Wilson, who had come to live with Mrs Tripp when her parents died. According to Roy, Mrs Tripp was a nice person who was very good to his family. Violette and Winnie remained friends until Violette went off to France on her second mission for SOE.

The Bushell children enrolled at Stockwell Road School. When Roy and Violette arrived back in England they were twelve and eleven years old respectively. Neither could speak English properly and so had to learn very quickly in order to get on with their lessons. They both spent a lot of their time at Brixton library trying to improve their English, which they soon managed. However, at home they often spoke French, much to the irritation of their father who never knew what they were saying. At school they were referred to as the 'frogs' and Florence Harwood, née

Cooper, a school friend who lived a few streets away from Violette, recalled that Violette's nickname was 'Froggy'. Florence remembered her as a very kind girl who would do anything for anyone and was a good friend to her, often protecting her from the school bullies. Her only complaint was that Violette insisted on calling her Flossie, which she hated. Florence's father had a motorbike and would sometimes give Violette a lift home from school. She loved to speed down Stockwell Road on the back of Mr Cooper's bike, her dark hair streaming out in the wind. Florence described Violette's hair as being like a raven's wing, so dark that it had an almost blue sheen to it.

In 1935 Reine gave birth to her last child, a boy named Richard. Their accommodation at Mrs Tripp's house was cramped at the best of times and with Richard's arrival it was impossible, so they found a new place to live with much more space at 18 Burnley Road, Stockwell. Here they had rooms in the basement, the ground floor and one room on the first floor of the house. Charles Bushell found regular work after the move and mellowed slightly now that the family income had stabilized. He grew vegetables in the small back garden and the family remained there, quite happily, until well after the Second World War.

Burnley Road is a residential road just off Stockwell Road. Today there is a blue plaque, placed on the wall of number 18 by the Greater London Council, which says,

VIOLETTE
SZABO.G.C.
1921–1945
Secret Agent
lived here
SHE GAVE HER LIFE
FOR THE FRENCH
RESISTANCE

In the 1930s the road probably looked much as it does today, as the houses were old even then. However, six and a half decades ago Stockwell Road would have been a very different place. Many of the buildings that were there then have been replaced with more modern structures and there are several housing developments that were not there in the 1930s. At the corner of Burnley Road and Stockwell Road was the London County Council Public Health Department Dispensary and next to that the Lambeth Borough Council Welfare Centre. There then followed a variety of businesses: a confectioner's shop owned by Thomas Lewis, Isaac Tasch's kosher butcher's shop, Arthur Bloom's bakery, a leather goods shop, an outfitters, Matthews' motor tyre factory, Miller's garage, Sidney Davis' second hand book shop, Nicholls & Co., printers, the L.C.C. Tramway sub-station, Brixton Estate Agency, the Old Queen's Head and Pride & Clarke Motor Car dealers. At the corner of Rumsey Road was a savings bank and on the other side of Stockwell Road was the school, between the Lambeth Divisional Offices of the London County Council Education Department and Mold's Furnishing Stores. A high, dark Victorian building, it is still a school and now has a garden dedicated to the memory of Violette Szabo. Another of its famous ex-pupils is the rock star David Bowie.

Just along the road from the school was the Plough Inn, where Charles Bushell used to go for a pint and a game of darts, and three doors away from the public house was a cigarette and sweet shop owned by Charles Dawton where, in later years, Violette used to buy her Churchman's No.1 cigarettes.

The children had a longer distance to walk to school once they moved to Burnley Road, but they had much more living space, which made up for the extra walk. Violette enjoyed school and worked hard. It was a struggle at first having to cope with the language difficulties, but she persisted with her studies and eventually did well. In later years she was remembered with affection by her teachers as being a lively and friendly child. Her experience of life up to that point was very different from that of the other children; she could speak another language and had lived in France. She could talk about things and places that most of them never imagined they would ever experience and, as children often do when confronted with someone different, they flocked around this exotic little girl.

Violette's favourite occupation at school was sport. She was athletic and was very good at gymnastics. She used to practise her acrobatics with her brother, Roy, turning handstands and climbing onto his shoulders. She took part in all the sporting events at school and did very well. With four brothers and a number of male cousins, it was no wonder that she was a tomboy.

She enjoyed music, listening to a variety of performers such as Charlie Kuntz, Gracie Fields and Joan Sutherland on the family's wind-up gramophone, and, for a time, had violin lessons, but these came to nothing and she soon gave them up. Roy thinks it was probably just a fad. He said of her, 'She was no highbrow, always cheerful, with a devil-may-care attitude.'

School holidays were spent apart, as the Bushell family never went away together. Roy and John spent most of their time in Hampstead Norreys with their grandmother or with Aunt Mabel. Violette stayed with her father's sister, Aunt Florence, and her husband, Uncle Harry, for most of her free time, although she also enjoyed visiting her mother's family in Pont Rémy in France.

Harry Lucas, who had been the landlord at the New Inn in Hampstead Norreys, had later moved and taken over a public house in Hereford. When he left the pub he got a job looking after the hounds for Mrs Simmons, who was Master of Foxhounds in Wormelow, Herefordshire, and he and his family moved to a house called The Old Kennels.

Aunt Florence and Uncle Harry had five children, Norman, Betty, Jean, Brenda and John; Norman and Violette were the same age and got along very well together. Violette used to play with the younger children and the other children in the village, climbing trees and teaching them to play games such as rounders in the surrounding fields. There are stories about Violette climbing out onto the roof of The Old Kennels and running along the ridge, but her cousin Norman thinks this was unlikely. The roof was very steep and Norman thinks it more likely that she climbed onto the roof of a lean-to that used to be attached to the back of the house.

The Lucas family lived in The Old Kennels until the end of the war when Mrs Simmons suddenly, and quite unexpectedly, gave them one month's notice and they had to move to a small house in Hereford.

Roy and Violette joined a cycle club, having purchased their bikes on the 'never-never' at two shillings a week. They used to meet up with other club members at a small café in Kensington and from there would cycle all over London and beyond. They often went as far as Runnymede where they stopped by the river and, if the weather was warm enough, had a swim or, if there was enough time, they went on to Pangbourne, a little Thames-side village to the north-west of Reading in Berkshire, a round trip of about 100 miles. Their brother, John, and his friend, Tony Phipps, sometimes joined them. They frequently cycled to visit their aunt, Annie Buckingham, and her family who lived along the Great West Road opposite to where Heathrow Airport now stands. In those days, before the airport turned the area into a bustling hive of activity, there was a lot of farmland and open fields to explore. Roy remembers this time as being their most enjoyable years.

Aunt Annie had six children, five boys and a girl named Violet. She and Violette were very similar in appearance, although Violet was older than her cousin. It was pure coincidence that both girls had different language versions of the same name. The Buckingham boys all loved Violette and she enjoyed their company. She was regarded by them as being one of the boys and could do anything they could, climbing trees, shinning drainpipes and scaling walls. She was a very good shot, winning all the prizes at the local shooting galleries. She also enjoyed boating and was a strong swimmer.

The Buckingham cousins were also close to the Lucas cousins and when Norman Lucas found himself a job in a garage at Sunbury on Thames all the cousins would get together at the Buckingham house and use it as a base for their excursions. Norman remembers walking across the fields to get back to his job in Sunbury after a day out at the Buckingham's. He told me of a local legend that there was a 'Treacle Mine' in one of the nearby villages!

Although family life in Burnley Road was, in general, fairly harmonious, Violette and her father often had differing views about a number of things and argued quite a lot. After one of their numerous fights, one day Violette decided she had had enough. Saying not a word to her parents, brothers or friends, she took her passport and a few clothes, packed a small bag and ran away from home. Somehow she got herself down to the coast and on to a cross-channel boat. When the boat docked in France she made her way to her Aunt Marguerite's house, but found that her aunt had gone away for a few days. Even this setback did not faze her and she set off to look for her aunt, whom she eventually found. Several days after her disappearance her anxious parents got the news that she was safe.

Her brother, Roy, has no idea how she made it all the way to France but he makes the observation that 'she was pretty smart and pigheaded!'

Chapter Two

Work and War

Violette Bushell left school in 1935 at the age of fourteen. There have been many references to the fact that she wanted to be a hairdresser and that the cost of her training was more than her parents could afford. This may or may not have been true. I have not been able to uncover any evidence to support this theory and Roy says that he has no recollection of her desire to be a hairdresser; but he did say that it is possible that it may have been something she wanted to do. Instead she went to work for a French corsetière in South Kensington. It was not the sort of job she enjoyed; it was far too dull and she did not like the restrictions imposed on her. Because she was the junior member of staff it was her job to attend to the others, fetching and carrying for them, bringing them their morning coffee and afternoon tea, sweeping the floors, dusting the shelves and generally making sure that everything was tidy. She also made deliveries to customers, which was the best part as it did give her a chance to get out for a bit, away from her boring surroundings. It was freedom of a kind and she was earning a small amount of money, but it was not what she had hoped for.

It was while she was working in Kensington that she had the argument with her father that sent her hurrying off to France. Her dissatisfaction with the job may even have been a contributory factor in her decision to go to France. When she eventually got back to England she found that she no longer had a job. In her absence she had been dismissed for taking unauthorized leave. Although she needed new employment it was a relief not to have to go to Kensington every day to a job she thoroughly disliked.

She began the search for something more appropriate. Her mother wanted her to become a dressmaker as she herself had been. She saw it as steady employment and a sure way to make a regular income. After all, people would always need clothes. It had certainly rescued the Bushell family during the times when Violette's father had been between jobs, but Violette fought against the suggestion. Traditional female pursuits were not at all to her taste; sewing, cooking and housework in general were tasks to be endured rather than enjoyed, and were certainly not something at which to make one's living.

Eventually Violette managed to find a position as a sales assistant in the Woolworth shop in Oxford Street, which was much more to her liking as she was not stuck in a boring backroom but was out, mixing with the public, with whom she had an easy rapport.

Her free time was still spent mainly in the company of her brothers and cousins, but sometimes she did go out with girlfriends, such as Winnie Wilson. They would go to Streatham to the Locarno where Violette loved to dance, often inventing her own dance steps. She also shared a love of ice-skating with her brother John. They often went skating at an ice-rink next door to Selfridges in Oxford Street and soon became quite expert. Roy went with them once or twice, but could never master the art and eventually gave up trying.

Thanks to their mother's dressmaking skills, all the Bushell children were well dressed. Although she was not interested in sewing, Violette loved pretty clothes made from brightly coloured fabrics. In summertime she often wore shorts, which were the most practical clothes for her sporting pursuits. One of her former neighbours in Burnley Road, Bett Bailey, née Starmer, remembers her wearing shorts with the bottoms turned up and a shirt, which she had partly undone and tied the loose ends in a knot, exposing her bare midriff. As Bett said, 'She was definitely ahead of her time'. Some of her friends' mothers thought she was a bit too daring, but she was just having fun and developing her own sense of style.

When Roy left school he went to work at the Savoy Hotel in the Strand. A dance was held every year for the staff and when he attended the party in 1937 Roy asked Violette to be his partner. Their mother made an evening dress for Violette, her first, which Roy described as being 'made of oyster satin and gold'. Violette looked absolutely stunning in her new dress and she arranged her hair in little curls on her forehead. She also wore a borrowed gold necklace of a typical Art Deco snake design. Roy was happy to be seen in the company of such an attractive girl, even if she was his own sister! Violette's first venture into the world of adult parties was a great success and she received a lot of attention from the other guests. She was even asked to dance by the General Manager of the hotel, who left Roy to dance with his wife.

Sometimes Violette went out with a boy who also lived in Burnley Road, but at number 10 on the opposite side of the road. His name was Albert and he was Bett Bailey's brother. He sometimes took Violette to the Astoria cinema close to where she used to live in Stockwell Park Walk. Bett and her friend would follow them and listen to their conversations and make fun of them while they queued to get into the cinema. When they came home they would say goodnight to each other just around the corner from 18 Burnley Road, in St Martin's Road, away from the Bushell parental eyes. Bett's friend lived very close to their favourite goodnight spot and would report to Bett how long it had taken them to say goodnight! When the friend and her family moved from the house in St Martin's Road, Bett and her family moved in and Bett could then watch and make fun of her brother herself. At one time Albert and Violette's initials were scratched into the brickwork of the wall against which they stood. No one knew which of them had scratched the letters and the wall was demolished long ago, with no trace remaining today of what may have been the record of their friendship.

Albert had a wind-up gramophone on which he liked to play a recording of *One Fine Day* from Madame Butterfly, sung by Deanna Durbin. It was a favourite of both Albert and Violette and he used to open the window and turn the gramophone up loud so that Violette would hear it from across the road. Sometimes, on Sunday mornings they would go off for a bike ride, often accompanied by Albert's friend, Tommy. Theirs was a happy, relaxed friendship but it was not a great romance. Roy recalls that she had other boyfriends, including one called Manny and another called

Sidney, but at that stage in her life she was not looking for a serious relationship.

Time marched on and with it came the threat of war. In 1939 Mr Bushell found himself a new job, working for a company called Rotax as a storekeeper. The company had become part of the Lucas group in 1926 and had some premises in Willesden, north-west London, where Mr Bushell went to work. The factory manufactured aircraft magnetos, generators and starters and other assorted aircraft parts. With the possibility of war, production was being increased and eventually the Willesden site expanded, taking over the neighbouring Vi-Spring Mattress factory in order to start production of the drive for the starter of the legendary Rolls Royce Merlin engine. Mr Bushell stayed at Willesden for three and a half years, before transferring to Rotax's new premises at Morden in Surrey.

Violette, in contrast to her father, had not yet given much thought to the impending conflict. She was having too much fun with her sporting activities, skating and dancing to worry about whether or not there might be a war. She certainly had no desire to join one of the armed forces at that point and when the Woolworth store in which she worked began laying off staff and she found herself unemployed again she began looking for another job. She was not out of work for long; she soon found a job much closer to home at the Bon Marché department store in Brixton Road. Here she worked on the perfume counter and was a popular member of staff both with her colleagues and with the customers, although her friend, Eileen Hughes, recalled that she didn't like working there very much.

She used to cycle to work along Stockwell Road, passing as she went the Matthews' Motor Tyre factory. A young man from the factory used to wave to her as she went by and they formed a friendship. His name was Sidney Matthews and his family owned the factory. He and Violette started going around together to restaurants and to parties. Sidney told me, 'She was a very pretty girl and great fun to be with'. They remained friends for the rest of Violette's life.

Sidney's family also had a factory in Cobham in Surrey that made breechblocks for Sten guns and the family home was in nearby Esher. The last time that Violette visited Sidney there must have been after she joined SOE. She came with a girlfriend and was wearing what Sidney described as a 'drab uniform'. Her ankle was strapped up and she said that she had sprained it. Presumably this was the accident she had had on her first attempt at the parachute course. Sidney owned a .22 rifle with a telescopic sight and they spent that last afternoon together practising shooting in his garden. Then Violette and her friend left and Sidney never saw her again. He only learnt later about her work with SOE and commented to me on the thoroughness of the preparations made by F Section. He had heard that Violette had had a gold filling put into one of her teeth, even though she did not need it filled, to make her appear more French.

When war was declared on 3 September 1939 Mr Bushell became an air raid warden and Roy joined the army. As soon as he was old enough John also went into the army; Roy thinks he joined the Royal Electrical and Mechanical Engineers (REME). By 1943, when he was seventeen years old, Noel, Violette's third brother, had also joined the armed forces. He served with the Navy and was part of the Pacific fleet, whose home base was Sydney, Australia. It was Noel's liking for his temporary home and the opportunities that it offered which led the rest of the family to emigrate to Australia in the early 1950s.

Violette was still not concerned with war work during the first winter of the war. It was the time that came to be known as the Phoney War when nothing much happened. For her nothing had really changed; people still wanted to buy perfume and she was still there to sell it to them. By the spring of 1940, however, things were going badly in Europe. The Germans invaded Denmark and Norway in April. After the death of a number of Danish resistance fighters, the government ordered the population not to resist and a non-Nazi coalition government was allowed to hold power. The Danish royal family, headed by King Christian X, remained in Denmark throughout the war.

Britain and France came to the aid of Norway. Ships were sent into Ofoten Fiord near Narvik and began bombarding the Germans. They, expecting a landing, began to flee, but Narvik was not captured as the Allied forces had only half a battalion ready for a landing. British, French and Polish troops also made an attempt to capture Trondheim, but were unsuccessful due to the lack of suitable equipment for the weather conditions and the continual air attacks by the Luftwaffe. The Norwegian army continued to fight and joined up with the small force that landed near Narvik. A second naval bombardment took place, after which land troops, including men of the French Foreign Legion, stormed Narvik and drove out the occupying Germans. However, before the town could be secured, events further south took over and the Allied troops were removed, allowing the Germans to re-enter the town. King Haakon VII and the rest of the Norwegian royal family fled to Britain and a pro-German puppet government under the Norwegian Nazi supporter, Vidkun Quisling, was set up.

Suddenly the Phoney War was over. On 10 May Winston Churchill replaced Neville Chamberlain as Prime Minister and on the same day German troops invaded Belgium, Holland and Luxemburg. Then they turned their attention to France and by the end of May the men of the British Expeditionary Force had been pushed back to Dunkirk. Then came Operation Dynamo, the miracle of the 'Little Ships'; the paddle steamers, cargo boats, ferries, fishing vessels, tugs, yachts and motor launches that came racing across the English Channel to snatch a total of 338,226 officers and men from the beaches and return them safely to England. Of this total, 139,097 men were French.

With the land of her birth now in enemy hands Violette decided it was about time that she did something for the war effort. She wanted to do something together with her friend, Winnie Wilson, so they joined the Land Army. Winnie had not been well and was not able to do anything very strenuous, so she and Violette were sent to Fareham in Hampshire to pick strawberries.

Many people in the villages of Locks Heath, Titchfield Common and Sarisbury close to Fareham made a living from strawberry growing. After the end of the First World War many ex-servicemen were able to buy plots of land, thanks to government subsidies, and so set up their own strawberry plots. Every year there was a great influx of outsiders to pick the ripe strawberries, including large numbers of gipsy travellers who regularly arrived every May. With the advent of war and the introduction of the Land Army, the Land Girls were seen as ideal for this task.

It was regarded as extremely important and a morale booster that there was a supply of little luxuries, like strawberry jam, in times of austerity.

Violette and Winnie had a reasonably pleasant stay, picking strawberries by day and visiting the pub for a drink and a game of darts in the evenings. But the pay in the Land Army was not very good and the girls only earned about £1-17s for a minimum fifty-hour week. By the time the strawberries had been picked and sent off to market, Violette had decided that the Land Army was not for her. She wanted to do something more directly involved with the war and went back to Stockwell to consider what else she could do.

Chapter Three

The Fall of France

By mid-1940 London had become a temporary home for thousands of French men and women who had escaped from their homeland when it was overrun by the Nazis. The Dunkirk evacuation in May and June 1940 had brought, not only retreating British soldiers of the British Expeditionary Force, but French fighters as well. More were arriving all the time and by the end of June they were rallying under the command of the relatively unknown General Charles de Gaulle as the Free French Forces.

On 14 July, Bastille Day, the first such holiday spent under Nazi occupation, the Free French held a parade in London. Violette's mother sent her off to watch the parade and see if she could find a homesick Frenchman to bring home for a meal and a few hours of friendly company. Winnie Wilson agreed to go with Violette and they left for the Cenotaph where the parade was being held. They found that the task was not as easy as they had supposed. It was just not possible to march up to a total stranger and invite him into your home without the invitation being misinterpreted. Eventually they met a member of the French Foreign Legion who stopped to chat to the girls and Violette was able to tell him of the task she had been set by her mother. The young man, 60145 Sergeant Major Etienne Michel René Szabo, was delighted to accept Mrs Bushell's invitation. It seems likely that he was more drawn by the idea of spending the evening with Violette than by the desire to spend an evening speaking French, but the offer of a home-cooked meal must have been appealing to him as well and he knew no one in London with whom to spend his free time.

Whatever the reason, he was happy to accompany the girls back to Stockwell, where he met Violette's family. His conversation with Mr Bushell was very limited and conducted mainly with signs, as neither could speak the other's language, but he managed to tell the family a little bit about himself.

He had only recently arrived in England. He was a member of the 1st Battalion of the 13 DBLE (13 Demi Brigade Légion Etrangère) which had been founded in Africa from among the Foreign Legion's African garrisons, and which had been in Norway. He was one of the legionnaires who had stormed Narvik and driven out the German Forces. When the Demi Brigade arrived back in Brest following their hurried departure from Norway they found they were too late to stop the German invasion of France and so the 13 DBLE departed for England to join the Free French forces. Not all Etienne's colleagues wanted to fight under the Free French flag. Only about half of them decided to fight alongside the British; the other half went back to their barracks in Morocco to join the Vichy troops. Etienne told them that he had only a few more days before he had to return to his camp in Hampshire and that he would soon be going overseas again.

All too soon the evening came to an end and Etienne stood up to leave. He thanked Mr and Mrs Bushell for their hospitality and when he said goodbye to Violette he asked her if she would meet him again and share what remained of his leave in London. She had much enjoyed his company and was happy to agree. Immediately they arranged another meeting and saw each other as much as they could until Etienne had to return to his unit.

A courtship ensued, carried on at a distance, as Etienne was stationed at Morval Barracks, part of the Southwood Camp at Cove, near Farnborough. Whenever his duties allowed he would come up to London and he and Violette exchanged letters at every opportunity. She introduced him to other members of her family and to her friends, who all called him Stephen, the English version of Etienne and much easier for them to remember.

Very soon Violette and Etienne began to talk of marriage. A meeting with Mr and Mrs Bushell was arranged and Etienne struggled with a mixture of signs, French and broken English to ask Mr Bushell if he might have Violette's hand in marriage. Her parents were shocked at the speed at which the courtship had proceeded. Violette was only nineteen years old and, although she had had plenty of friendships with boys, there had been no one who could have been described as a serious boyfriend.

Etienne was eleven years older and much more worldly wise than Violette. He had spent much of his life in the Foreign Legion and had travelled a good deal. Unfortunately details of his early life are very sketchy. I have been told that he was born in Hungary and came to France as a seventeen-year-old boy specifically to become a legionnaire. Someone else told me that it was his father who came from Hungary and that Etienne was actually born in France. I asked his daughter, Tania, about him and she said she knew very little except that he came from Marseilles and had been orphaned quite early in his life. On his marriage certificate he was shown as being a thirty-year-old bachelor, son of a French policeman, also called Etienne Szabo. When I asked Roy what he could tell me about him he said:

> Etienne I only met twice, and knew nothing about him apart from his marrying my sister, but he seemed a nice enough fellow.

I was finding it impossible to get any information about Etienne the person rather than Etienne the soldier, and then I was unexpectedly given the address of one of his cousins. I wrote to him immediately. In his reply he said that the only knowledge he had of Etienne was second-hand and had been passed from one member of his family to another. Because he had no first-hand knowledge he didn't think there would be anything useful for my book and he told me that all the people who had passed on this information were now dead. I wrote back to him and told him of the difficulties I was having in trying to find anyone who could tell me anything about him and said that if he could think of anything at all to tell me, even if I had to report that it was hearsay, I would be grateful. His reply was immediate and unexpected. He said:

> Lots of water passed since, under the bridges of the Danube, the Seine and the Thames Rivers. Bygones are bygones and

certain matters shall be forgotten until the necessity arise and/or really important historical events will require them to be remembered. Neither is the case today.

He continued by making mild threats about what he would do if I contacted him again. I was shocked by his extreme reaction to a perfectly polite request. It left me wondering if I had disturbed some skeleton in the family cupboard or whether he was merely embarrassed about his lack of knowledge of his more famous kinsman.

It soon became obvious to Mr and Mrs Bushell that Violette was determined to marry Etienne, whether or not she had their approval. Since Violette was technically a minor and would require parental consent for the marriage they realized that if they withheld it they would have a fight on their hands. They liked Etienne and did not relish the idea of an argument with their stubborn daughter, so they gave their permission for the marriage to go ahead.

On 21 August 1940, a Wednesday, Violette Bushell became Mme Violette Szabo at Aldershot Registry office. The wedding took place by special licence and Mr F.A. Ruff, the registrar, married the couple. Violette's parents and her brother Roy, who was stationed in Aldershot at the time, were at the ceremony and Etienne's best man was one of his colleagues, Lieutenant Etienne Kiss.

R.J. Minney in *Carve Her Name with Pride* gives a detailed description of the attendance at the wedding of General Marie-Pierre Koenig, later to be the celebrated commander of the 13 DBLE and subsequent commander of the État Major of the French Forces of the Interior (EMFFI). At that time Koenig was not yet a general, but Minney describes how the 'General' kissed both bride and groom and then turned his attention to the mother of the bride. Mr Bushell, it was said, was nervous about the possibility of being kissed also and was relieved when the 'General' merely shook his hand. I asked Roy Bushell if he knew how Koenig came to be at the wedding of a sergeant major when he himself was of a much higher rank. Roy, who attended the wedding himself and can be seen in the wedding photo, told me, 'General Koenig was not present,' and, as one can see from the photo that Roy kindly sent me, there was no one there who even vaguely resembled him. The person who has sometimes been described as being Koenig was, in fact, the best man, Etienne Kiss.

After the ceremony Violette and Etienne went off to a small hotel nearby for their honeymoon. They only had one week in which to begin to get to know each other properly. Their courtship had been mostly conducted at arm's length and in any case they had only met five weeks before the wedding. If Etienne had not known that he was to be posted overseas, perhaps they may have delayed the wedding for a few weeks, but the knowledge that he would shortly be out of the country had prompted them to marry almost immediately.

All too soon the week was over and Violette said goodbye to her new husband and went back to Burnley Road in Stockwell. Etienne went up to Liverpool to join his colleagues of the 13 DBLE aboard the Dutch ship SS *Pennland* for the long voyage to West Africa. Their ship was one of a convoy, in which there were a number of British ships, including the battleships HMS *Barham* and HMS *Resolution*, aircraft carrier HMS *Ark Royal*, four cruisers and sixteen destroyers. Travelling on another Dutch ship, SS *Westernland*, was General Charles de Gaulle and Churchill's representative, Major General Sir Edward Spears. This ship flew the Cross of Lorraine, emblem of the Free French Forces. The task of the 13 DBLE was to try to force the Vichy French in West Africa to change sides and support the Free French under de Gaulle. De Gaulle, who was convinced he would be able to win over the Vichy French, had formulated the plan, but it had the full backing of Winston Churchill.

The convoy left Liverpool docks on the last day of August and made its way out into the Atlantic Ocean, the journey made so much longer than normal by the necessity of avoiding German U-boats. After a voyage lasting about two weeks, the Free French forces sailed into harbour in Freetown, the capital city of Sierra Leone. They remained there for a week before setting sail once more, this time for Dakar in Senegal. They arrived off the coast of the Senegalese capital on 23 September and heard the news that several French colonies had sworn allegiance to the Free French. These included Chad, Cameroon and Equatorial Africa. It gave them renewed hope that they would be able to fulfil their task.

Contrary to de Gaulle's expectations, however, the Vichy troops in Dakar put up a fierce fight. The Governor-General of Dakar, who had been appointed by the Vichy government, had received strict orders not to surrender. De Gaulle's broadcast, appealing for surrender, was ignored and when emissaries were sent ashore they were promptly arrested. The British ships fired in support of de Gaulle, but were met with counter-fire from both the shore and from the French battleship *Richelieu*. HMS *Barham*, two cruisers and two destroyers were hit and HMS *Resolution* was crippled after being hit by a torpedo from the submarine *Bévéziers*. Any attempt by the French at a landing in Dakar was abandoned and Churchill ordered the troops away from Senegal.

They returned to Freetown from where they left to sail to Douala in French Cameroon and then onwards to Libreville in Gabon. Here Marie-Pierre Koenig, whose career had been steadily progressing, led a troop against the Vichy forces who were successfully defeated within a matter of hours. Koenig was promoted to Colonel in recognition of his victory in Gabon.

The men of the 13 DBLE went back to their ship and began the long journey down the Atlantic west coast of Africa, round the Cape of Good Hope and up the coast of South Africa until the ship reached Durban.

Back in Stockwell, Violette was restless. She didn't have a job, as her husband preferred her not to work, but she had nothing with which to fill her time. She was bored and didn't know what to do. One day merged into another. The only time she looked forward to was when the postman delivered the mail and she received something from Etienne. He was the same prolific letter writer he had been during their brief courtship, sending her dozens of letters, also writing postcards to her young brothers, cousins, aunts and uncles. Of course the mail was heavily censored and they weren't allowed to know where he was, but they could make informed guesses by the hints he dropped and from listening to news bulletins on the wireless.

By the time Etienne was on his way to Durban Violette had had enough of the quiet life. She felt that she just couldn't sit and do nothing while her husband was risking his life for his country. Not wanting to upset him by taking a permanent job, she applied for a temporary position as a telephonist at an exchange near St Paul's. The Post Office, who provided the telephone service in those days, took on many temporary staff during this period and there were always vacancies for new recruits. Violette worked in the exchange all through the London Blitz. Then, on 29 December 1940, the Luftwaffe dropped 10,000 firebombs on the City of London. The raid was timed to coincide with low tide on the Thames, making the task of the fire service more difficult. When water supplies became short the 20,000 fire fighters who had attended the blaze, assisted by soldiers and civilians, had to try to pump in the water from the river, an almost impossible task at low water. The whole of the City seemed to be on fire; only the black silhouette of St Paul's Cathedral stood out against the orange and red flames. One of the casualties that night was the telephone exchange where Violette worked. She was not there at the time and so escaped injury, but the building was gutted and the telephonists, thanks to Reichsmarschall Herman Göring, received an unexpected holiday while new premises were found.

Once more Violette found herself with nothing to do, but this situation did not last long as temporary accommodation was found for the telephone exchange in a damp cellar close to where it had been before. Again Violette began to feel that she should be doing something more productive than being a switchboard operator, which she felt was not very important.

1941 arrived. Etienne Szabo and his colleagues were by now making their way up the east coast of Africa, through the Indian Ocean, round the Horn of Africa and through the Gulf of Aden into the Red Sea where they docked at Port Sudan in mid-February 1941. They went south to the village of Suakin where they camped until the end of the month. Then they began the overland journey into Eritrea where they were to take part in a number of battles against the occupying Italian forces along with British and Commonwealth soldiers.

The British and Commonwealth troops had been fighting near to the town of Keren, but had become stuck. They had to get through a huge rock cliff, which bordered Keren to the west and stretched for many miles to the north and south of the town. There was only one narrow passage through this rock, the Dongolaas Gorge, and the Italians had blocked the gorge and were encamped at the top overlooking the Allied troops. The RAF began a bombing campaign against both Keren and the port of Massawa. Fierce fighting between the ground troops ensued and by the end of March the Allies had managed to clear a passage through the Dongolaas Gorge. They pushed on and were met by the Anglo-French Force from Port Sudan, which included the 13 DBLE, under the command of Brigadier Harold Briggs. On 1 April the Eritrean capital, Asmara, fell to the Allies and then, on 8 April, so too did the port of Massawa.

At the beginning of May the Free French Forces once again boarded their ship and set sail up the Red Sea for Suez. From Suez the 13 DBLE went on through the Sinai Desert and into Syria where they fought against the Vichy troops who controlled the northern part of the country, pushing them back as far as Damascus. It was a sad time for the 13 DBLE for there were members of the Légion Etrangère fighting with the Vichy forces. It was here that Colonel Marie-Pierre Koenig took command of 13 DBLE following the resignation of Colonel Magrin-Vernerey, also known as Colonel Montclar. Eventually, at the end of June, the Free French took Damascus from the Vichy troops, but in the victory parade that followed were surprised to find the population regarded them as traitors rather than liberators.

Back in England Violette had taken a break from the monotony of the telephone exchange and had gone to Wormelow to visit her Aunt Florence. In the fresh air and pretty countryside her flagging spirits began to revive and the persistent cough which she had been unable to shake since working in the damp cellar began to get better. Her cousin Norman was also at home on a few days' leave and the pair had a wonderful time chasing round the narrow lanes on Norman's motor bike. Soon it was time for Norman to rejoin his ship and, reluctantly, Violette also packed her bags and returned to London. The time away from home had given her a chance to think and she was more determined than ever to do something positive in the struggle against the Nazis. She decided that she must join one of the women's forces and thought that the

Auxiliary Territorial Service (ATS) was the one for her. Now all she had to do was convince her husband.

At the end of August Violette received a telegram telling her that Etienne was on his way back to England. Hurriedly she packed her case and caught the train to Liverpool. It was just over a year since they had last seen each other and the week they had together was like a second honeymoon. Then, as with the first honeymoon, the time flew by and suddenly Etienne was on his way back to North Africa. Violette made the long train journey south from Liverpool to London and returned to her parents' home in Stockwell to wait for Etienne's next leave.

Although Etienne would have preferred his wife to remain at home, he could see that she was unhappy and had reluctantly agreed that she could join the ATS if that was what she really wanted. She went straight to the recruiting office when she got back to London and on 11 September 1941 became Private Violette Szabo of the Auxiliary Territorial Service.

Chapter Four

1942

The Auxiliary Territorial Service came into being on 9 September 1938 by a Royal Warrant, signed by HM King George VI, which said:

> Whereas we deem it expedient to provide an organization whereby certain non-combatant duties in connection with our military and air forces may from time to time be performed by women:
>
> Our will and pleasure is that there shall be formed an organization to be designated the Auxiliary Territorial Service.

Before the war was over, both the King and the Prime Minister would become closely involved with the ATS when their daughters, Princess Elizabeth and Mary Churchill, both joined. Princess Elizabeth, now Queen Elizabeth II, became a driver in the ATS and is said to have been very enthusiastic about her duties, discussing in great detail over dinner with her parents the workings of a car engine.

It is doubtful if, even after expressing a wish to be treated the same as all other recruits, the then Princess Elizabeth had to suffer the same primitive conditions that most girls had to endure. Recruits had to be tough to survive. Their living conditions were primitive and they were thrown together and had to get along, regardless of their diverse backgrounds. The uniforms issued to them did not always fit and they had to make them do so very quickly as there were countless parades and kit inspections. These alterations were done with the aid of something called a 'housewife', which was a standard-issue sewing kit.

Violette dreaded being assigned to some sort of domestic task. There were many occupations that would not have suited her at all: cooks, orderlies, bakers, tailoresses or mess stewards to name but a few. Then she discovered that she might be able to work in a mixed (male and female) heavy anti-aircraft battery. That was much more to her liking as it would involve the same work as the men. The only thing that women were not allowed to do was to fire the guns.

Having completed her basic training, Violette was sent to Oswestry in Shropshire for her specialized training. Up to the mid-part of 1942 there were three such training regiments in Oswestry, but the ATS specialist unit was the 7 Heavy Anti-Aircraft Training Regiment. Specialized training took some weeks to complete and included a practice exercise at another camp. Then a period of leave was granted. Violette went back to Stockwell, to Burnley Road, and had a good rest. Then, on 18 December 1941, she assembled along with the other members of the battery at the station ready to form part of the defences in the north of England. The battery commander was reported as saying that this group of trainees was great and that, when told to assemble at the station, they all did so exactly as ordered with no absentees except one young man who, during his leave, had come down with scarlet fever.

Violette was part of the 481 HAA Battery which itself was part of the 137 HAA Regiment. The battery commander was Major J.W. Naylor. He was a regular soldier who had been on the point of being posted overseas when illness prevented it. The alternative was to be sent to command a mixed heavy anti-aircraft battery. Major Naylor was very disappointed at first in having to look after a mixed group but eventually came to regard them all with affection and respect.

When setting up a mixed battery it had been decided to divide it into three groups. The first group consisted of the officers, the Battery Sergeant Major, the Quartermaster Sergeant and about twenty bombardiers and gunners who were already experienced in the work that had to be done. The second and third groups were composed of male recruits from a Royal Artillery training regiment and female recruits from an ATS training centre, who had all completed basic military training but knew nothing else. The latter two groups were then trained together on the use of the equipment at a heavy anti-aircraft battery. The first group of soldiers attended a refresher course while waiting for the others to get up to speed.

Some of the girls who were being trained found it hard to get along in a mixed battery. There were those girls who had spent their entire lives thus far in the company of females, having had nannies or attended all-girl schools. Violette, of course, was completely at home in male company, having spent her childhood and teens with an assorted bunch of brothers and, mostly male, cousins.

She found her work on the predictor interesting and enjoyed being part of a team which was performing a vital task. When firing at a moving target such as an aeroplane, it was important to try to judge where the target would be when the missile reached it and to aim for that point. Merely aiming at where it was when first spotted would ensure that the missile missed and the aeroplane survived to fight another day. It was a difficult task, as they had no control over what the enemy aeroplane would do and the missile did not have a constant speed. It would leave the gun very fast but its speed would diminish depending on the distance or angle it had to travel. To take the guesswork out of firing required a lot of teamwork.

The first piece of information that was required was the height of the aeroplane. This was done with a height finder, which was a long tube with a telescopic sight at each end and an eyepiece in the centre with a small hand wheel. The person operating the height finder would, at first, see two images of the aircraft, which, with the aid of the wheel, could be made to merge into one image. Having done that the height of the aeroplane could be read off from a scale along the tube.

The next step was to send the height of the target to the predictor, a large metal box, which changed the present position to a future position and gave the time it would take for a missile to reach its target. The whole thing was a complicated process.

The guns had to be trained ahead of the target and kept ahead by means of a dial on which there were two pointers representing the target and the missile. The fuse setter then had to predict the time it would take to set the fuse and to load and fire the gun, which would tell him the actual time to call for the gun to be fired. Five people, each working together as a team and each depending on the other for correct information so that they could ensure their own part of the process was correct, operated the predictor.

The first mixed battery was deployed in Richmond Park and received a lot of attention. There were problems foreseen, not least the question of who would be in command of the women, the male officers or those of the ATS. It was felt by some women that ATS soldiers might be able to hoodwink male officers by using feminine charms and that a woman would be able to control the females better. Eventually this silliness was forgotten as the soldiers, both men and women, formed themselves into teams who mostly worked extremely well together.

Between April 1941 and July 1942 just over 12,000 women were selected to become predictors. The only selection that was larger was that for mess orderlies, which accounted for 13,323 women. It was found that women were as good as men in predicting and that they were better than their male counterparts when it came to height finding. The only section in which the men beat them was in initial spotting. This is perhaps not so surprising when one considers that most little boys can identify aeroplanes whereas little girls usually cannot. The men therefore had an inbuilt advantage over the women in this task.

The men who manned the heavy anti-aircraft batteries were soldiers of the Royal Artillery and, as such, were known as bombardiers and gunners instead of corporals and privates. With the mixed batteries it was decided that while on duty the women could also be known by these ranks instead of the regular ATS ranks. Thus, while she was working her predictor, Private Szabo was known as Gunner Szabo. ATS girls working with Royal Artillery regiments were also allowed to wear the grenade badge on their uniforms with the AA Command formation sign on their sleeves. Their regular ATS lanyards were also replaced with the white lanyards of the Gunners.

Gunner Szabo proved to be a popular member of the battery

who fitted in well with her colleagues. She worked hard but was always at the forefront when it came to play and took part in all the entertainment put on by the members of the battery. On one occasion she performed her own version of belly dancing, which concluded with a spectacular back somersault that, much to her embarrassment, caused part of her costume to fall off. In her more serious moments she volunteered to teach French to her colleagues.

Violette's ATS career had hardly started when she discovered she was pregnant. She continued working at the battery for as long as possible but it was in reality only for a few weeks and when it became impossible for her to continue with her duties she obtained her release from the service and went back to her parents' home to await the birth of her baby. She was sad to leave and promised everyone that she would return once the baby was born. Quite what Etienne would have thought of that has not been recorded. Violette continued to write to him at every opportunity, although his replies often took a long time to arrive. When he heard about the baby he was delighted and said that he would try very hard to get back to London in time for the birth.

Violette, with Etienne's agreement, decided that she should find a flat that would be their first home together. Curiously the place she found was in London, where there was still a danger of German air raids, rather than in the country where it would be safer for a new baby. But, had she moved to the country she would not have had the support of her family nearby and, if Etienne were to manage to get leave, it was much easier for him to reach London than to have to make his way to some unfamiliar country area.

The flat that Violette found was at 36 Pembridge Villas in Notting Hill, London W11. It was part of a large house, with a basement, that had been converted into flats in 1937. There were five flats in all, over five floors including the basement, each with one bedroom except that on the third floor, which had two bedrooms. All the living rooms looked out towards the street. I have been told by someone who visited her there that Violette's flat was on the first floor, although I have not been able to obtain any written proof that this was so. The entrance to the flat was opposite the stairs and opened into the living room, which was about sixteen feet wide and thirteen feet long. From there a door in the same wall led to the bedroom, which was approximately ten feet wide and thirteen feet long and looked out to the back garden. To the side of the bedroom window were several steps, which led down into what was described as a lobby, in reality a tiny hallway. Straight ahead was the bathroom and to the left was the entrance to the kitchen, which was alongside the bathroom. All the one-bedroom flats were of a similar layout and dimension.

In the absence of someone coming forward with proof that they rented a flat to her, it is almost impossible to establish conclusively which one of the flats was Violette's. I contacted the Land Registry to try to find out who owned the flat on the first floor during the time that Violette is said to have lived there. Surprisingly, they were not able to tell me. Apparently they only register leases of twenty-five years or more. Although 36 Pembridge Villas was converted to flats in the late 1930s, the first time the flat on the first floor was registered was in June 1975, which means that all leases before that time were very short-term.

Notting Hill was under the jurisdiction of Kensington and Chelsea Council who issued the rates books for the owners or tenants. Both the basement flat and the flat on the second floor seem to have officially changed hands during the war as the names on the rates records for both these properties have been changed. Violette is unlikely to have lived in the basement as the records show that for two months in the middle of 1943 the flat was empty. When it was again occupied the name of the person shown on the records corresponds with that on the first electoral register issued after the war and on subsequent electoral registers. Likewise the second-floor flat also changed hands in 1941, but thereafter remained in the same name until the end of the war. And so it would appear that the flat in which Violette lived from 1942 until 1944 was the one on the first floor, as I had been told.

This flat was registered in the rates records under the name Pietro Bel Giudice for the entire period of the war. I had no luck in finding any information about this man until I discovered that his name had been spelt incorrectly. It should have been del Giudice and not Bel. Once I found the correct spelling I also began to find details about the man. He was an Italian national who, at the start of the war, had been imprisoned in the Isle of Man as an enemy alien, thus leaving his flat empty. At that time internment was the fate of most Austrians, Germans and Italians living in the United Kingdom. If they weren't actually imprisoned they were certainly considered for internment and had to satisfy the authorities that they did not pose a threat to national security. Most of the Italians who were imprisoned were sent to camps on the Isle of Man. Some of the other so-called 'Enemy Aliens' were sent as far away as Canada or Australia.

Unlike many of the Italians sent into detention during the war, Pietro del Giudice was not a waiter, confectioner or a shopkeeper; he was a Doctor of Law. Born in Rome on 2 April 1904, he was the son of a lawyer. His elder brother, Filippo, also a Doctor of Law, had come to the United Kingdom in 1933 and started his own law practice, handling mostly cases concerning nationality and domicile problems. In 1936 Filippo was engaged by Ludovico Toeplitz, an associate of the film maker Sir Alexander Korda, who needed advice on Italian law after an injunction had been brought to prevent Hollywood star Bette Davis making a film in Italy. A friendship ensued which culminated in the formation of the film production company, Two Cities Films, with Filippo acting as legal adviser.

When I first met Tania, Violette Szabo's daughter, we spoke about the fact that her mother had, at one point in her short life, been a film extra. Tania had been told about this by her grandparents but did not known which films she had been in. We talked about how wonderful it would be if we could find out and be able to watch her in a film. Discovering that the owner of the flat in which she lived had a brother involved in films made me wonder if, perhaps, she had found the film work through her landlord or, conversely, if she had found the flat through her film work. Unfortunately I don't have the answer. What I did find out was that Filippo del Giudice was a very well respected film producer who worked on films such as *The Way Ahead*, *This Happy Breed* and Laurence Olivier's *Henry V*. It was he who, in 1940, persuaded Noel Coward to both write and star in the enormously popular film based on the story of Lord Louis Mountbatten's ship HMS *Kelly*. The film, which was called *In Which We Serve*, opened in 1942 to enthusiastic reviews and earned two Oscar nominations and a special award to Noel Coward for his 'outstanding production achievement'. It may be fanciful on my part but there is a scene in the film set at a railway station where two couples are saying goodbye. In the background is a young, dark-haired woman. As the camera moves she turns her head and for a second you can see a face that could be that of Violette Szabo. Then she is gone and you are left wondering if it could really be possible.

As Violette settled into her new home and began the last few weeks of waiting for the birth of her baby, Etienne was also waiting, in far less comfort, in the desert outpost of Bir Hakeim.

During the first few months of 1942 there had been a period of inactivity in North Africa. It was to be the calm before the storm. General Erwin Rommel used the time to re-equip his forces and then began a push towards Tobruk. The 1 Free French Brigade, which included nearly 1000 legionnaires of the 13 DBLE, was sent to the Western Desert where it joined a division of the Eighth Army to assist the British and Commonwealth troops who were trying to hold back the German advance. The Allied defensive line was known as the Gazala line, starting as it did from the coastal village of Gazala in Libya. It consisted of a long line of barbed wire fencing and minefields, interspersed with manned posts known as 'boxes', the most southerly of which was at Bir Hakeim and was manned by the Free French Forces under General Marie-Pierre Koenig.

The conditions at Bir Hakeim were extremely primitive. Although there was supposed to be an abandoned Italian fort there, in reality it was just a random collection of derelict concrete buildings on a small plateau. There was very little else. The British troops who handed it over to the French had made an underground city of dugouts and trenches in which they lived like rabbits, covering the holes with anything they could find. It was stiflingly hot. Sometimes there was no wind at all; at other times it would blow ferociously and whip up a blinding sandstorm. The heat of the day gave way to freezing nights and there was a constant shortage of water both for drinking and for washing. What little water there was had to be brought by tanker from

Tobruk and was desalinated seawater, which was very unpleasant to drink.

It was here, in these inhospitable conditions, that Etienne and his colleagues waited for over three months. To the south was nothing but the sands of the Sahara and to the west were the advancing troops of the Afrika Korps. If Rommel had decided to break through the Gazala line on his way to Tobruk their wait would have been for nothing, but, although there was some fighting on the northern sector of the line, the main body of German troops headed south for Bir Hakeim in an attempt to go around the line of defence.

The German assault on Bir Hakeim began on 3 June 1942. German troops started clearing a narrow passage through the minefield under cover of Luftwaffe attacks from above. The aerial attacks lasted for a week and were almost non-stop – 1300 sorties in total. In addition to the Luftwaffe attacks, the French were being attacked on the ground by tank troops of the 90 Light Division. Although the British tried to relieve the French positions their armoured brigades did not manage to get through and the French were left alone to defend Bir Hakeim.

On 8 June 1942 at St Mary's hospital in Paddington, Violette and Etienne's daughter, Tania Damaris Désirée Szabo, was born. She was a small, dark-haired baby, who looked very much like her mother. As soon as she was able, Violette sent word to Etienne that he had become a father.

On the day that his daughter entered the world Etienne Szabo was suffering one of his worst days so far in the desert. The French were being subjected to constant bombardment from both ground and air and, as the day wore on, German ground forces came within yards of the French soldiers, only to be beaten back once more. Rommel was impressed by the tenacity of the French and said of their fierce defence that day:

> This was a remarkable achievement on the part of the French defenders who were now completely cut off from the outside world. To tire them out, flares were fired and the defences covered with machine-gun fire throughout the following night. Yet when my storming parties went in the next

> morning, the French opened fire again with undiminished violence. The enemy troops hung on grimly in their trenches and remained completely invisible.

Luftwaffe attacks continued. The French had almost completely disappeared beneath the ground but had left their wounded in tents clearly marked with red crosses. The Luftwaffe pilots ignored the crosses and bombed the makeshift hospital, killing the wounded and destroying their meagre medical supplies.

Rommel sent three ultimatums to Koenig demanding that the French troops surrender. Koenig ignored them. On 10 June the Afrika Korps again pressed forward under cover of artillery and air attacks, breaking through the northern French defences. Rommel then sent in the 15 Panzer Division with orders to rout the French troops by the following day. Unknown to the Germans, the French forces had decided to break out of Bir Hakeim that very night and under cover of darkness managed to get the majority of their troops out through the one gap left in the German lines. In vehicles and on foot the men picked their way through the minefields and the clusters of German troops until they were eventually clear of the enemy. When the 15 Panzer Division bombarded the encampment the next day, before entering it to take the French surrender, they found that, apart from a handful of wounded French soldiers, Bir Hakeim was completely empty.

In spite of the courage of the French troops and the delays that their fight at Bir Hakeim had caused the Germans, Rommel's forces stormed ahead and eventually took Tobruk. It was a severe setback for the Allies and a personal blow for Etienne Szabo. Having survived the carnage at Bir Hakeim in which a third of his colleagues had been killed, Etienne was desperate for some leave. He only learned of the birth of Tania after he had reached safety and was anxious to meet his daughter as soon as possible. All his letters to Violette spoke of his delight at becoming a father and of his desire to return to England as soon as he could.

The weeks and the months went by without any sign of his leave being granted, until in October his chance of meeting his daughter and seeing his wife again was lost for ever. On the evening of

23 October the Battle of El Alamein began with the firing of 1000 Allied heavy guns directed towards Rommel's troops. Under cover of this fire, Allied soldiers moved through the German minefields clearing a path for the infantry and tanks to follow. Within fifteen minutes the guns were silent again. Then, five minutes later, they began firing once more, even more fiercely than before. To the south of El Alamein the Free French Forces had been deployed to create a diversion on a mountain called Qaret El Himeimat. On one side of the mountain was a gentle incline occupied by German and Italian troops armed with machine guns; the other side was an almost vertical rock face. The French action began in the early evening of 23 October with the troops approaching the rock face across a plain littered with mines. From the top the Germans and Italians fired on them. When they finally reached the rock face they were expected to climb it and overwhelm the enemy forces at the top. They had been set an impossible task. Trapped at the bottom of the rock with much of their equipment destroyed by enemy fire, many of the French were killed. The rest had to withdraw to rethink their position. In the early hours of the next morning a second group of French soldiers charged at the rock and managed to climb it and overwhelm the Italian forces at the top. However, they too had to withdraw rapidly before the advancing German tanks overtook them. Retreating to the foot of the cliff they tried to regroup but were fired on continually by the Germans at the top. Huge numbers of them were killed and injured and they eventually had to withdraw across the plain, taking their injured with them in ambulances.

It was during this horrific action in support of the Allied effort at El Alamein that Etienne Szabo was badly injured. He was said to have shown great courage and a complete contempt for the danger he faced in leading some of his men into action on the morning of 24 October. Then, while being evacuated, he was mortally wounded in the ambulance that was taking him to safety. I have not been able to discover if his fatal injury was the result of enemy fire or an exploding mine but the result was the same. He died a hero, at the age of thirty-two, never having met his little daughter.

The Allies fought on, pushing the German troops back. Rommel is said to have exclaimed in frustration, 'Rivers of blood were poured out over miserable strips of land which, in normal times, not even the poorest Arab would have bothered his head about'.

By the beginning of November Rommel planned to retreat but was told by Hitler:

> Yield not a metre of ground and throw every gun and every man into the battle. Your enemy, despite his superiority, must also be at the end of his strength.
>
> As to your troops, you can show them no other road than that to victory or death.

However, in spite of Hitler's rhetoric, on 4 November the Germans began retreating and the Battle of El Alamein was won by the Allied forces.

It took some time for Violette to learn of the fate of her husband. She continued to write long letters to him, describing Tania in great detail. She had found a place for the baby at a nursery run by Mrs Margaret Edwardes in Havant in Hampshire. Mrs Edwardes was the wife of a naval officer and the nursery was set up to look after the children of service personnel. Presumably Violette was able to send Tania there because of her own ATS service. The house was called Yew Tree Lodge. After the war it was sold to the Portsmouth Water Company and was demolished in 1966 to make way for their new office buildings.

Violette was kept busy travelling back and forward from London to Havant to see her baby and, at first, was not worried about the lack of letters from Etienne. There had been a lot of news about the fighting in North Africa and, although she didn't know his exact location, she knew that he was somewhere in Africa. As the weeks passed, she began to be concerned. She tried to find out what had happened to him, but no one seemed able to give her an answer.

Finding the travelling down to Hampshire both tiring and time-consuming, Violette decided to bring Tania back to London. Instead of taking her to the flat in Pembridge Villas, she arranged to have her looked after by Miss Vera Maidment who lived at 59 Fernside Avenue in Mill Hill, NW7. She, herself, did go back to the flat to wait for news of Etienne. She was bored and restless.

In spite of her attempts to find out what had happened to her husband she received no news. One day, when visiting her parents, her father spoke to her about what she was doing with her life. Although she had a baby, because Tania was living away from her in Mill Hill, she was not a full-time mother and Mr Bushell wondered whether she might like to do something to keep her mind off her worries about Etienne. He had recently transferred from the Rotax factory in Willesden to the new facility in Morden in Surrey. This factory was regarded as a model factory, employing as it did blind, deaf and other disabled people under a new Ministry of Labour rehabilitation scheme. It was involved with the manufacture of aircraft switchgear and, said Mr Bushell, was a good place to work. Although it was regarded as being in Morden its actual location was close to South Wimbledon tube station so it was relatively easy to reach. There were a number of factories in a small industrial complex there and Rotax had taken over a building that at one time housed the British Sewing Machine Company. The factory still exists and is now used by BOC. Mr Bushell told Violette that there were a number of vacancies at the factory and she eventually decided to try it. Anything was better than sitting at home worrying about what had happened to Etienne, and Violette applied herself to the job with great enthusiasm. She did so well that she was soon promoted but her work at the Rotax factory was cut short when she eventually received the shattering news of Etienne's death.

Violette was inconsolable. She felt hurt and angry and cheated. She had spent so little time with her husband and now he was gone. He had not even met their child before his death. She felt unable to work any more and left the factory. Gradually she began to cope, but the anger remained and with it came a hatred of the nation that had robbed her of her husband. She was consumed by the desire for revenge. Everyone told her that time was a great healer but as time passed her anger at the Germans and her hatred for them remained. She decided that, whatever it took, she had to do something to avenge her husband's death.

Chapter Five

SOE

It has been said that when Violette Szabo received a letter from a Mr E. Potter requesting her to attend a meeting in his office, she believed it to be about the pension she expected to get following the death of Etienne. It was, in fact, her call to SOE, the Special Operations Executive, set up at the behest of Winston Churchill to 'set Europe ablaze'.

Before the start of the war discussions had been held in various quarters about both the possibility and the desirability of setting up a group which would function in much the same way as the subversive groups known to exist in Germany and Italy. Three organizations developed, each with its own ideas of the most important areas of subversion; D Section of the Secret Intelligence Service (SIS), Military Intelligence (Research) MI(R), headed by Colonel John Holland, and Electra House (EH), under the direction of Sir Campbell Stuart.

D Section appointed Major Laurence Grand, of the Royal Engineers, to formulate a plan. This he did and made his first report in May 1938, setting out a number of targets which he considered suitable for sabotage activities. These included agriculture, communications, transport and supplies, and also something curiously referred to as 'moral sabotage', which was a form of propaganda.

The function of MI (R) was, broadly speaking, to liaise with other departments within the War Office, the Technical Research branch and other Commands, into the problems of tactics and organization, under the direction of the Deputy Chief of the

Imperial General Staff (DCIGS). However, he is quoted as saying, 'I have introduced a research section directly under me. This section must be small, almost anonymous, go where they like, talk to whom they like, but be kept from files, correspondence and telephone calls'.

Electra House was set up in January 1939 to address the problems of propaganda to enemy countries, distributing misinformation that could not be traced back to the British government.

It soon became clear that the causes for which these organizations were working would be better served by the formation of a single unit covering all functions of the three separate groups. There was much discussion during the first half of 1940, which culminated in a request from the Prime Minister at the beginning of July, to his predecessor, Neville Chamberlain, then Lord President, to research the subject and to report back. This he did with great speed, his report having been delivered to Hugh Dalton, Minister of Economic Warfare, before 16 July. The organization, which it recommended should be established, would be headed by Mr Dalton, who was formally asked by Churchill to accept the position of Chairman on 16 July. Mr Chamberlain's report was distributed and approved by the War Cabinet on 22 July and became the formal Charter of SOE (see Appendix A).

In June 1940 the Germans invaded France and on 16 June the French Prime Minister, Paul Reynaud, resigned and was succeeded by Marshal Henri Pétain, hero of Verdun, who formed a new government in Vichy and asked the Germans for an Armistice. The day after Reynaud's resignation General Charles de Gaulle, who had also seen service at Verdun, left France for England from where he broadcast to the French people the following day, saying:

> I, General de Gaulle, invite French officers and soldiers who are on British territory or who are coming here, with or without arms, to join me. I also invite engineers and workers who are experts in the arms industry to join me. Whatever happens, the flame of the French resistance must not go out and it will not go out.

By 22 June an Armistice had been signed and five days later de Gaulle, now firmly established in London, formed his Provisional French National Committee, being recognized the following day by the British government as the leader of all Free Frenchmen. Pétain severed diplomatic relations with Britain on 5 July and on the 11th was made both President and Prime Minister, assuming the title Chief of the French State.

On 8 August General de Gaulle was sentenced to death *in absentia* by the Vichy government. At the same time Georges Mandel, former Minister of the Interior, General Gamelin, who had been Army Commander, and ex-premiers Leon Blum and Edouard Daladier were all arrested and charged with causing the defeat of France. France was in turmoil and it was time for the fledgling organization, SOE, to go to work on its behalf.

Major Leslie A.L. Humphreys, who had been D Section's representative in Paris, formed the French section of SOE in the summer of 1940. In December he moved on to explore ways of communicating with France through Spain and Portugal, and a civilian, H.R. Marriott, who had represented the textile company, Courtaulds, in Paris, took his place. A year later he relinquished his position to Major Maurice Buckmaster who was to remain head of F Section until it was closed down, with the rest of SOE, in January 1946.

In May 1941 a new French section, known as RF Section, was founded. Where F Section was composed of agents, quite often half English and half French who had been recruited by the British, RF Section was run by the British but worked with the Bureau Central de Renseignements et d'Action (BCRA), its agents being recruited by the Free French and with direct connections to the French Resistance. Although they were both working for the same result, there was often friction between the two sections. This was a situation probably exacerbated by the attitude of the Free French leader to anyone not directly under his control. When, after the liberation of France, de Gaulle was introduced to an F Section agent who had worked long and hard for its deliverance, he did not congratulate the man or thank him, he merely looked at him and said, 'Go!'

Major, later Colonel, Buckmaster went to work at the Baker Street office that SOE had acquired in October 1940 and had named the Inter-Services Research Bureau. In civilian life Buckmaster had been an executive of the Ford Motor Company in Paris and was a committed Francophile. He also had a deep commitment to his agents and watched carefully their progress both in Britain and, later, in the field. He had the last word concerning the recruitment of agents for his section and often overruled decisions made by instructors about an agent's suitability. In spite of his concern for the people under his command, he was not an easy man. Those who knew him at the time have described him as both anti-social and unapproachable, a man in an ivory tower.

Maurice Buckmaster's assistant in F Section was a thirty-four-year-old woman, who was to become a legend in SOE. Born in Romania in June 1907, Vera Maria Rosenberg came to England in 1933, where she settled with her parents in London and adopted her mother's maiden name of Atkins. She had been to school in France, attending a number of establishments across the country and completed her education at the Sorbonne in Paris. Consequently she spoke flawless French and was well acquainted with French manners and customs. Maurice Buckmaster quickly saw the value she would add to his department. She was single-minded and self-opinionated but she brought an enormous amount of energy and dedication to her work. It has been said that one section head described Vera Atkins as, 'the most powerful personality in SOE', and she was certainly regarded as a formidable character but, unlike Buckmaster, she was approachable. Although she had her favourites among the many agents who passed through F Section, in a sense she was a friend to them all, looking after personal matters for them, sending messages to their families while they were away, escorting them to the airfield prior to their departure for France and, when the war was over, finding out what had happened to the ones who didn't return.

Agents were recruited into SOE in a number of ways. Vague advertisements were sometimes placed in newspapers asking for French speakers to contact the War Office. Those who responded usually expected to be offered war work as translators; some had their names submitted by the service in which they were already enlisted and agents and other employees of SOE put forward names of those they felt might be suitable. The interviewers had a delicate task, finding out a candidate's suitability without disclosing too much of what would be asked of them.

Security was a huge problem; without it the organization would cease to function properly and so it was imperative that no information about the nature of the organization be disclosed at an early stage. Once a candidate had been selected for training, it was necessary to create a cover story for family and friends. Female agents became members of the FANY, the First Aid Nursing Yeomanry, a civilian voluntary organization founded before the First World War. FANYs were employed in a number of different jobs from canteen workers to prison guards, in clerical positions and as drivers. Becoming a member of the FANY provided a plausible reason for being away from home and allowed them to undergo the specialist training required of an agent without awkward questions being asked by family and friends.

Mr E. Potter was the assumed name of Selwyn Jepson, a forty-four-year-old writer. The son of the detective author, Edgar Jepson, he had been educated at St Paul's School in London and at the Sorbonne in Paris. He served in the Tank Corps during the First World War and then, following in the footsteps of his father, became a mystery writer himself, producing a long list of books including *The Qualified Adventurer*, *That Fellow MacArthur*, *The King's Red-Haired Girl*, *Snaggletooth* and *Love in Peril*. In 1950 his book *Man Running* was turned into the Alfred Hitchcock film *Stage Fright* which starred Marlene Dietrich and Richard Todd. As well as being a successful author, Jepson was a particularly effective interviewer who recruited many agents into SOE.

There has never been a conclusive answer to the question of how Violette Szabo came to be recruited. Neither her brother Roy nor her cousin Norman can shed any light on the matter and, as Duncan Stuart, SOE Advisor at the Foreign & Commonwealth Office, told me, the amount of material on her personal file is 'lamentably slight'. It is possible that she came to the attention of SOE through having been in the ATS. The French conversation lessons that she gave then would certainly have alerted her officers to the fact that her language ability might be of further use. There is, however, a document located in SOE files, but not in Violette's personal file, which adds to the mystery. It is a memo sent to Captain Jepson from E. Alexander, on 20 July 1943, which says:

> Georges Clement, who left today to go into the field, has given me the following name and telephone number as a possible recruit for the organisation: Mrs. Czabo, Tel: Bayswater 6188.
>
> He mentioned that the lady had already applied to the Belgian Section but had been told to wait a month, which she did not wish to do.
>
> He asked that his name should not be mentioned when contacting her.

Next to the name 'Czabo' someone has written by hand, 'Already seen as "Szabo" '. Jepson may have written this, as Violette had already been given a security clearance on 1 July 1943 and on 10 July it had been decided that she would be trained as an agent in the field. She may, indeed, have been interviewed for the Belgian section and told to wait for a month. That, however, seems unlikely as suitable agents were always needed and, having already passed a security check, it would surely be unusual to ask one to wait for a month.

The use of the word 'applied' is also puzzling. SOE was supposed to be a very secret organization. Elaborate procedures were adopted to ensure that there was no hint of its real activities, including misleading and ambiguous name plates outside office buildings and the use of apartments and other residences, which had been acquired under assumed names for the purpose of interviewing and training agents. So how would Violette have known that there was a section to which she could apply? Certainly not by casual knowledge of the organization, and, if it had been through an existing member of SOE, that would surely have indicated a serious breach of security. The memo does not indicate any concern that Violette had spoken to Georges Clement, and yet a member of the public, for that is what she was at that time, discussing the possibility of covert work with someone already engaged in that pursuit must surely have rung alarm bells. She may, of course, have been found through other means, but at the very least it would seem to indicate that Violette was acquainted with existing members of SOE who thought she would be a suitable candidate for undercover work, not realizing that she had already been recruited.

The identities of those named in the memo have not shed any light on the mystery. It is possible that 'E. Alexander' was Margaret Eilean Alexander, the daughter of Lieutenant Colonel William Arthur Alexander OBE, who was employed as a secretary in F Section and who was in charge of administration and registry at the SOE premises at Orchard Court. Lieutenant Georges Clement was a twenty-six-year-old officer in the 3rd Hussars, part of the Royal Armoured Corps. He was from a White Russian background, having been born in Petrograd (now St Petersburg) in 1917. He had been educated at the Imperial Service College in Windsor and at Brasenose College, Oxford, and spoke fluent French, having lived in France for ten years. He was recruited into SOE in February 1943 and trained at STS5, Wanborough Manor, STS52, Thame, and STS36, Boarmans at Beaulieu. In July 1943 he parachuted into France as wireless operator for the Butler circuit in the area around Le Mans. He operated successfully until 28 November 1943 when he was arrested by the Germans in the middle of transmitting a message to London. He was held for a time in the prison in Rennes before being transferred to Fresnes prison outside Paris in the spring of 1944. When he left Fresnes it was to be deported to Germany from where he was sent to Mauthausen concentration camp, near Linz in Upper Austria. He was executed at Mauthausen on 6 September 1944.

In his 1956 book *Carve her Name with Pride* R.J. Minney said that Selwyn Jepson interviewed Violette in a sparsely furnished room in Sanctuary Buildings. I have not been able to find any other reference to Sanctuary Buildings with regard to SOE or to any other agents. The accounts of others, including that of Maurice Buckmaster in his 1952 book *Specially Employed*, mention only an anonymous hotel room and Duncan Stuart has said that, as far as he is aware, Sanctuary Buildings was not among SOE's properties. Wherever it was that this interview took place, Jepson supposedly told her that he thought her knowledge of

French might be put to good use in a covert role. She is said to have asked if he meant as a spy, probably thinking of the spy stories she liked to read as a child. He told her that was not quite what he meant but did say that it could possibly involve unconventional or dangerous work. Violette apparently jumped at the chance to serve in this way. This may or may not be true. Unfortunately, there is no longer any written record of this conversation, if, in fact, a record ever existed. Minney also said that Violette hid the fact that she was a mother from Jepson and that he felt that, had he known at the time that she had a child, he would not have recruited her.

On Violette's personal file Tania is certainly not mentioned in the section listing her relatives; that part states only:

> Father – British, In England.
> Mother – French, In England.
> Widow of Frenchman (French Legionnaire)

However, a memo dated 4 September 1943 and sent by Vera Atkins to Captain Bourne-Patterson, Planning Officer and deputy to Buckmaster, reads:

> Mrs SCABO (sic)
> You have probably not yet met this woman who is a new and fairly promising trainee. She has a one-year-old child and is very anxious to know, at once, what pension arrangements would be made for her in the event of her going to the field.
>
> Provision for her child is such a primary consideration to her that I am sure she feels unsettled about her training and future until this question has been dealt with. I told her that she would no doubt be entitled to the pension payable to a service woman of her rank i.e. Section Leader, but I wish we could give more precise assurance to our women agents with children.

This not only seems to suggest that, from the earliest stage of her time with SOE, were they aware of Tania's existence, but that they knew there were other mothers within the ranks of SOE agents.

Yvonne Cormeau and Odette Sansom, for example, were both mothers and were recruited well before Violette.

As with the initial selection processes, training also brought to light security problems. Some prospective agents, judged as being entirely suitable at their interviews, proved to be the exact opposite once their training commenced. It was not possible just to return them to civilian life or to their former military positions, however, as they knew too much about SOE and its organization. It would appear to be the case that some agents were allowed to continue with the training and were eventually sent into the field rather than waste the time and effort that had been spent on them, but this was both foolhardy and dangerous.

A partial solution was found by the establishment of the ISRB Workshops at the SOE site in Inverlair, Invernessshire, where unsuitable students could be occupied until the importance of their knowledge became less significant. Inverlair was unique, as it was the only one of SOE's facilities that housed students of all nationalities under the same roof. The site at Inverlair functioned for thirty months until it was finally closed in February 1944. The candidates who had been deemed as unsuitable were kept busy producing, among other things, climbing equipment, which was used by the Norwegian section of SOE. Each Monday the men (there were no women at Inverlair) were allowed to spend the evening at Fort William and there was never a problem with this concession. The men were referred to as 'malcontents', but that was a misnomer as they were just ordinary men who were either physically or mentally incapable of completing the training that would qualify them as agents. Strangely enough, there were men at Inverlair from all the country sections except France. This is particularly curious when one considers the size of the French section. It would appear that once a man had been selected for training by the French section his destiny was set; regardless of his suitability, he became an agent. It would surely have been better for some of these poor souls to have spent the war making climbing equipment.

It was decided that it would be better to have a way of weeding out unsuitable candidates before they acquired any sensitive knowledge. Accordingly, in June 1943 the Student Assessment

Board (SAB) came into being with a country house, Winterfold, which was given the designation STS7 and was situated in the village of Cranleigh in Surrey. Here the students went through both practical and psychological tests, designed to prevent unacceptable students from being placed on courses teaching subjects of a covert nature. The SAB replaced the Preliminary Schools and seems to have been very effective in its purpose. It was to Winterfold that Section Leader Violette Szabo of the First Aid Nursing Yeomanry came to begin her assessment on 7 August 1943, completing it on 27 August.

It would appear from Violette's initial report that Vera Atkins had been correct when she stated that she thought Violette might feel unsettled about her training and future as her results were not as good as one would have expected. Her Morse training and performance was rated as average, as was her mechanical ability; her intelligence rating was 5 but in the general agent grading she only rated a D. Nonetheless, the remarks on her report at the end of the course noted that she was:

> A quiet, physically tough, self-willed girl of average intelligence. Out for excitement and adventure but not entirely frivolous. Has plenty of confidence in herself and gets on well with others. Plucky and persistent in her endeavours. Not easily rattled. In a limited capacity not calling for too much intelligence and responsibility and not too boring she could probably do a useful job, possibly as courier.

There is a note on her personal file which says, 'Country Sect. We agree remarks on SAB report'. 'Country Sect.' refers to F Section and after this positive endorsement it was agreed that she should be sent to Group A at Arisaig in the Scottish Highlands for her paramilitary training.

There were ten country houses which had been requisitioned by SOE for use by their students as Special Training Schools in the district of Arisaig and Morar, providing accommodation for approximately seventy-five students in groups numbering no more than six to eight at a time. The small groups ensured that students could be given individual attention. In the early days of its existence the course lasted about three weeks. However, this was later extended to five and, on occasion, to as much as eight weeks.

Violette's file shows that she went to STS24 which was composed of the Lodge at Inverie and the smaller Dower House of Glaschoille, both of which were on the Knoydart peninsula and could only be reached by boat from the fishing port of Mallaig, a journey of about one hour. Lord Brocket, who was believed to be a Nazi sympathizer, owned the estate, of which these houses formed a part. He was not in residence during the time that the school was based there but had tried to visit early on in its occupancy, and although, as a member of the House of Lords, he held a pass which allowed him to enter Protected Areas, when he reached the control post at Corpach he was turned away and it was made clear to him that his presence was not welcome.

While trying to discover the exact nature of the training carried out in the Scottish Highlands I corresponded with and spoke to Aonghais (Angus) Fyffe. He not only had command of the Lodge at Inverlair, he was also Security Liaison Officer for the training schools in Scotland with responsibility for the security of all the SOE establishments there. These included the ten STS of Group A, three STS near Aviemore with the Naval training and departure outstation at Burghead on the Moray Firth, the Signals Station in Belhaven School near Dunbar in East Lothian and an office in Edinburgh which housed a detachment acting as a link with Scottish Command. Major Fyffe was also Chief Security Officer Military Operation No. 1 (Special Planning) Scotland and in that capacity was the link between SOE and all Naval, Army, Air Force, Police and Civil authorities in connection with exercises and operational rehearsals throughout Scotland. This also included the US Air Force base at Edzell, south-west of the village of Fettercairn, home to one of the country's oldest distilleries which produces a fine single malt whisky, Old Fettercairn, a favourite of Queen Victoria.

Aonghais Fyffe was almost certain that Violette stayed at the Lodge at Inverie, although no note was made of it on her personal file. He very kindly offered to send me details of the paramilitary training carried out by Group A at Arisaig and I reproduce his account here in full as it explains very clearly the nature of the training that Violette would have undergone during her stay in

Scotland. He began by stressing that all trainees, whether male or female, were treated in the same way:

> There was no distinction between the sexes and all suffered the same rigours of physical training in the early hours of wintry mornings, the same mud, muck, soakings in peat bogs on fieldcraft and the same sore muscles and aching joints from the Arisaig form of unarmed combat. After all, when they were crawling flat to the ground over the peaty marshes of Loch nan Uamh, they were all just 'bods in battledress'.

The Arisaig courses covered the following subjects:

- Physical Training including preparatory exercises for parachuting
- Silent killing
- Weapons training, including foreign weapons from 1942
- Demolition training
- Map reading and compass work
- Fieldcraft
- Appreciations; planning of exercises and operations
- Raid tactics
- Elementary Morse training
- Schemes designed to make use of the above

Physical Training

This was carried on, usually in the early morning, out of doors in all weathers, sunshine, rain, sleet, snow and with severe frost on the ground. It also included going over an assault course, which included the use of rope work in various forms and preliminary parachute exercises. These consisted of jumping from a height, learning how to fall properly with a forward roll and also to jump from a mock fuselage in the same way.

Silent killing

There were several books on unarmed combat but the silent killing method taught at Group A was a much more aggressive form and was intended to have a lethal outcome. It was constantly pointed out that when it came to a one-to-one fight with the enemy, only one of the two involved would walk away; so – make sure that ONE is YOU. The course also included knife fighting, which is not simply a matter of grabbing a knife and plunging it downwards; it is much more scientific and quite an art when properly practised. The various highly lethal spots on the human body were highlighted and the use of the hand was all that was necessary. Trainees fought with one another in some of those exercises but the more dangerous ones were practised on special dummy bodies where jabs and thrusts could be used with impunity.

Weapons

The use of the Sten gun was taught and, later, also of the Thompson sub-machine gun, but the main offensive weapon was the automatic pistol, either the .32 or the .45 calibre. The method taught was 'instinctive shooting', that is without the use of the gun sights. It was stressed that when one threw up an arm with finger extended to point at an object, that object was in direct line of sight; a pistol in the hand was simply a substitute for the finger. In the initial stages standing targets were used and the order 'Fire' meant immediate reaction against the target, when points were scored. But mock buildings were set up with separate rooms to give practice in close-up shooting, and stalking courses were set up where 'dropping' and 'pop-up' targets required immediate reaction. From late 1942 Major Sykes, the weapons instructor, decided to encourage the use of the .45 pistol at ranges of 80 to 100 yards, at which that handgun is still deadly, and ideal for taking out a sentry or guard with minimum noise.

Demolition

This covered the use of explosives, incendiaries and timing devices such as time pencils. This was a highly practical course and special 'mock-ups' of buildings and other likely targets were built to allow the practical use, and result of real charges. It was essential that trainees accustom themselves to the handling of these highly dangerous substances and gain sufficient confidence to enable them to make use of them safely when required to do so later in the field. Scattered widely over the Arisaig area there are still, today, relics of those demolitions courses here and there.

Map reading and compass work

Trainees were taught to make full use of maps to find their way about the mountains and glens of the Arisaig area, and the ability to use a compass properly was essential. They were also taught to memorize routes as they moved along so that, if they lost their map and compass, they could still find their way.

Fieldcraft

This was an essential part of the trainee course when they were taught how to move about the country unspotted and how to use natural cover and surroundings to approach their target unobserved. It almost always involved, at some point, crawling on their stomachs over wet, marshy ground and through smelly bogs. It was a really messy part of the course but a true test of physical stamina and mental concentration under stressful conditions.

Appreciations; planning reports and orders

The setting out of reports and orders was quite an important part of the instruction, intended to cut out unnecessary details and circumlocutory phrasing. Ultimately a standard pro forma was evolved which was used as far as possible.

Raid tactics

Trainees were taught to move about the countryside in small groups or formations to make raids on particular targets. This was mostly based on the subversive and guerrilla methods used in the minor wars in Europe in the pre-1939 years as, for example, in the Spanish Civil War.

Elementary Morse

This formed only a small part of the trainee course at Group A and was given merely to test the trainee's aptitude and to give a rudimentary knowledge of the sending and receiving of messages. Each was expected to attain an average speed of eight to ten words per minute each way. Advanced training was given to selected trainees at a later stage in the appropriate Signals Schools.

Schemes and exercises

Raids were planned against 'mock-up' targets, which could be attacked without material or property loss. There were also attacks on a railway siding and on the main line in which dummy charges and fog signals were used (often by night) and the local railway, the West Highland Line, cooperated by providing an engine and coach to add realism and practical experience to these exercises. There was also a course of para-naval training at Group A but this was short-lived when parachuting became the more usual means of infiltrating agents, as opposed to the early method of using a submarine or other sea-going craft.

It would appear that Violette began her paramilitary course around the beginning of September 1943 and on 7 September was assessed for the first time. The name of the person making the report is, unfortunately, not legible, but it is likely to have been her Conducting Officer or, perhaps, a Security NCO. Surprisingly, the opinion given was not good. It stated that:

> I seriously wonder whether this student is suitable for our purpose. She seems lacking in a sense of responsibility and although she works well in the company of others, does not appear to have any initiative or ideals. She speaks French with an English accent.

Two weeks later a further report was made by the same person, who highlighted the difficulties he was having in deciding on the suitability of Violette as an agent, as she displayed such contradictory characteristics. The reasons for this behaviour will, obviously, never be known. It may be that she was still concerned about proper provision being made for Tania in the event of her death and, of course, she was still mourning the loss of her husband, who had been dead for less than a year when this report was made. What it, and the subsequent report, shows is that Violette Szabo was an ordinary, albeit extremely pretty, young girl. She wasn't some super-heroine of whom great things were expected; she was 'the girl next door' who, nonetheless, when the time came, found within herself the strength and courage to do great things, against all expectations. The report, dated 21 September, says:

> For this member of the party one's feelings are bound to be mixed. Character difficult to describe:– Pleasant personality, sociable, likeable, painstaking, anxious to please, keen, mature for her age in certain ways but in others very childish. She is very anxious to carry on with the training but I am afraid it is not with the idea of improving her knowledge but simply because she enjoys the course, the spirit of competition, the novelty of the thing, and being very fit – the physical side of the training. She is very kind-hearted, although conceals it. The main reasons for stating in my previous reports my doubt regarding her suitability for this work are:–
>
> 1. When taking over a party, the first thing I concentrate on is to win the students' trust, friendship and encourage them to ask me questions concerning their future work. Although I am absolutely sure that she has not the faintest idea of what is going on the other side, she does not seem to bother to find out in the least, which in my opinion is a very bad sign. I put this down to (a) does not realize the implications of the work. (b) lack of foresight. (c) fatalistic mind.
> 2. She seems to be uncertain of her own mind and to have no definite purpose.
> 3. Has no initiative; is completely lost when on her own. Owing to her friendly disposition she has always had someone who took interest in her and on whom she could rely upon.
> 4. Speaks French with an English accent.
> 5. She is very temperamental, ranges from enthusiasm to depression for no apparent reason at all.

> However, I must admit she is rather a puzzle, (to the instructors as well) she has proved to possess certain qualities which I never would have expected her to have, and for this reason I consider it advisable for her to carry on with the training. She is quite reliable.

There is, of course, the possibility that Violette did not ask questions about what she was likely to encounter because she did not want to know in too much detail what life might be like on the other side. She had a strong determination to succeed and may have been nervous to know too much in case that knowledge shook her resolve.

At the end of the paramilitary course a final assessment was made which recommended whether or not the agent should be sent into the field. Violette's final report was made on 8 October and states:

> After a certain amount of doubt, especially at the beginning of the course, I have come to the conclusion that this student is temperamentally unsuitable for this work. I consider that owing to her too fatalistic outlook in life and particularly in her work, the fact that she lacks the ruse, stability and the finesse which is required and that she is too easily influenced; when operating in the field she might endanger the lives of others working with her. It is very regrettable to have to come to such a decision when dealing with a student of this type, who during the whole course has set an example to the whole party by her cheerfulness and eagerness to please.

It is peculiar that Violette should have received such a negative assessment, as her instructors were impressed with her performance. Major Sykes, the weapons instructor, is said to have held her and her ability in high regard. The damning report ultimately had no effect, as Violette was passed on to Group B for further training. On 12 October 1943 a memo was sent to a member of the Military Training staff which said:

> This student is nominated for the course at Group B commencing 17.10.43. Unfortunately it is too early to

> indicate the area in which she will be working as a courier. She will require 3 weeks plus scheme. She is bi-lingual in French and English.

The following day a memo from the office of the Director of Counter Espionage was received which said, 'Is still under consideration'. Even at this stage it is likely that they were considering whether or not she should be sent into the field. However, the same day, 13 October, STS headquarters notified Group B that Violette would be attending the course at STS 32c commencing 17 October.

STS 32c was one of the so-called finishing schools on the estate of Lord Montagu, at Beaulieu, in Hampshire. It was situated in a house called Blackbridge, to the north of the tidal section of the Beaulieu River. Blackbridge was the home of Lady Chamberlain, widow of the former Conservative party leader, Sir Austen Chamberlain, but the house had been rented to the Honourable Mrs Murray before being requisitioned by SOE.

It is interesting to note the criteria applied to the search for suitable properties. The following quote is taken from a document that I found at the Public Record Office entitled *Properties Section History*, which appears to have been written in March 1946 and says:

> It was stipulated that these houses for the Training Section must be secluded for Security reasons and that a relatively high standard of comfort and domestic services (heating, lighting, baths and W.C.s) must be provided.

The notion of what constituted a 'relatively high standard of comfort and domestic services' would, today, be regarded as very basic facilities. For some house owners with suitably secluded properties, the war provided an opportunity for them to upgrade their homes and ensure that they were well maintained at no cost to themselves. The time it took from requisitioning until the property was suitably adapted was, on average, eight weeks. As the war continued and more and more young men enlisted in the armed services, it became more difficult and, indeed undesirable, to use civilian labour for the refurbishment of these properties and accordingly at the end of 1942 a mobile construction unit was set up. It was called MCU77 and its complement came from the Royal Engineers. It had its headquarters in Chalfont St Giles, in Buckinghamshire, and was authorized to draw both RE and other Army stores and, whenever necessary, it was also permitted to obtain stores from the Ministry of Works and by local purchases which were financed by SOE funds.

In his book *Beaulieu: The Finishing School for Secret Agents* Cyril Cunningham tells how the syllabus for the Beaulieu course was based on training given at the MI wing at Arisaig and also that of D Section's training school at Brickendonbury Hall in Hertford. The course taught at the latter establishment had been, to a large extent, the work of master spies Kim Philby and Guy Burgess. Philby became an instructor at Beaulieu where, it was said, 'his performance as the principal instructor on propaganda warfare was regarded by his superiors, his fellow instructors and his students as outstanding'.

All the subjects taught at the finishing schools were in modular form so that the courses could, to a certain extent, be personalized and arranged to suit a particular agent's needs. The instructors were a very diverse bunch of men, ranging from the aforementioned spies to convicted burglars and a gamekeeper from the Royal Estate at Sandringham.

Sadly no record remains either of Violette's stay at Blackbridge or of her performance at the finishing school. She would, however, have been taught subjects such as the recognition of German military uniforms, the organization of the Gestapo, the planning of reception committees to receive either agents or supplies, the use of *Eureka*, a radar device which could guide an aircraft from a distance of twenty miles, and of S-phones which allowed agents on the ground to talk to airborne pilots; it was also important for agents to know how to choose sites which would be suitable for aircraft to land and take off. Other modules explained how the BBC sent coded messages during French news broadcasts, how codes worked, the coding and decoding of messages and how to escape if caught, for example the freeing of oneself from handcuffs. There was also instruction in fieldcraft, building on what had already been learnt in Scotland and explaining how to survive off the land by catching and killing one's own food. After the tough physical activity at Arisaig, Beaulieu must have seemed very different. However, although much of the course was classroom-based, it was extremely hard work.

Sometimes the exercises were conducted away from the finishing school. Agents learnt evasion techniques by being shadowed by instructors around local towns such as Bournemouth, Southampton or Portsmouth. They also practised shadowing other trainees in and out of department stores in the towns. There were other, longer exercises where they were given tasks to carry out such as removing sensitive material from, say, a factory site and bringing it back to Beaulieu without being apprehended by the police who would have been tipped off to look for the thief. These exercises, which were called schemes, could send the agent to anywhere in the United Kingdom. It was often necessary for them to find their own accommodation, meet up with persons unknown to them, sometimes simply by using a password and then finding the means of transport to get back to the school within the time allowed.

Violette's course lasted until sometime in the middle of November. Having completed the finishing school all that remained was to learn to parachute jump. She had to make two attempts at this part of her training as the first time she sprained her ankle on landing and was sent off to Bournemouth to convalesce. A photo of Violette in a wheelchair, which was taken while she was convalescing, shows her wearing a suit but no coat and the sun is shining. It is likely that R.J. Minney in *Carve her Name with Pride* was correct when he said that she made her first jump sometime between the courses at Arisaig and Beaulieu. Parachute training normally took place at this stage in an agent's training, but, as none of the dates Minney gives for Violette's various training courses coincide with the dates shown on her personal file, it is difficult to know whether or not it did take place then. There is no reference in Violette's personal file to her first parachute jump, except in the report of her second parachute course, which she began in late February 1944.

Bett Bailey, Violette's neighbour in Stockwell and sister of her former boyfriend Albert, remembers seeing Violette when she came home following her parachute accident. A young couple called Ada and Joe Hopkins lived in Burnley Road on the opposite side to the Bushell family home. One day Bett and Ada had been shopping and had trudged home with heavy shopping bags. Joe was at home but had remained in his armchair while Ada and Bett struggled up the steps with their heavy bags. The two girls were worn out and sat down to recover with a cup of tea. While they were sitting in the front room, which overlooked Burnley Road, Joe suddenly leapt from his chair and rushed outside. Ada and Bett went to the window and saw Joe run across the road towards the limping figure of Violette Szabo. He took her small case from her and put an arm round her shoulder to support her as he escorted her home. Having performed this chivalrous deed Joe went back home and finished his tea. He could not understand why Ada was annoyed with him. It had not occurred to him to help his own wife with her heavy bags but the minute he had seen Violette he had rushed to her aid. Bett said that Violette had that effect on people, especially men.

Parachute training was conducted at Ringway airport, Manchester, and students were sent to one of two properties in the area. Violette went to STS 51a, the address of which was Dunham House, Charcoal Lane, Dunham Massey, Altrincham, Cheshire. The school was commanded by Major C.J. Edwards MBE. Before attempting any jumps, students were taught how to fall correctly. One method used was a large slide, similar to those in children's playgrounds but much steeper. There were also harness-like contraptions in which the students could be strapped and which simulated the sensation of a parachute descent.

When the instructors were sure that the students were ready, they made their first jump from a balloon, jumping through a hole in the bottom of the basket. Most of them did not enjoy this; it was too still and quiet and, without the noise of the aircraft engines, didn't give the impression of what an operational jump would be like. Violette completed her course on 25 February when the following report was made:

> This student had previously visited the school and made one descent, spraining her ankle on landing. On her return she still seemed to be as nervous as she was on her first visit, but

> after making her first descent she gained confidence and carried out the remaining descents with verve. She carried out the ground training in good style, having difficulty only with the landing training. On all three descents, one from aircraft and one from balloon by day and one by night from balloon, her exits were good. On her first landing she parted her feet slightly and on her second she brought her knees up to her chest. These points were brought to her notice and she seemed fully to appreciate their danger, especially if she were to jump in any wind.
> THREE DESCENTS SECOND CLASS

And so, with this final part of her training complete, Violette was now considered to be ready to go into the field as a fully-fledged agent.

Chapter Six

The Salesman Circuit

In the early days of SOE the task of placing agents in occupied territory was a rather hit and miss operation. The first agents went by boat, but it was difficult to find places that were suitable to moor boats away from the prying eyes, not only of the Germans, but also the *Milice*, the Vichy-backed French police force. It was also difficult to get suitable vessels in the first place. The Royal Navy was less than enthusiastic about tying up a submarine and its crew just for the sake of one or two agents being landed in enemy territory, even though, from the point of view of SOE, submarines were probably the most suitable vessels.

After the fall of France a number of Frenchmen had arrived in England in fishing boats and SOE sought to use some of these boats to return to France carrying agents on board. But this project was short-lived. As soon as they had collected together a number of these fishing boats the Germans banned their use and would only permit French fishermen to use open-topped, small, coastal vessels in the Channel. It was, therefore, impossible to disguise them as part of the French fishing fleet.

Eventually most agents were taken to France and returned to England by aeroplane. Early parachute drops were often wildly inaccurate, as, without navigational help from the ground, even the most experienced pilot could sometimes lose his way. In the later stages of the war they were helped by devices such as the S-phone, which enabled agents in the reception committees on the ground to talk to the pilot and give him directions to the chosen landing field or dropping ground.

There remained the problem of taking agents out of France. Some went by land, using buses, trains, bicycles or foot to make their way through the French countryside down to the Spanish border. From there they had a long and dangerous trek through the Pyrenees and, having got through to Spain, risked arrest by the Spanish authorities. If they managed to get there without any problems they then had to be taken out of Spain, either by air or by boat, usually through Lisbon in Portugal or Gibraltar. It was a journey that could take many days, sometimes weeks, to accomplish.

An aeroplane that could take off and land in a very short space, and that had sufficient range to get to France and back without needing to be refuelled, was what was needed. The solution to the problem was found in the shape of the Westland Lysander. Developed in the mid-1930s as an army cooperation aeroplane, the Lysander was found to be too big and too slow for its original purpose when compared with enemy aircraft. It only came into its own when used by two special squadrons for transporting secret agents to and from mainland Europe. The aircraft were Lysander Mark IIIs and Mark IIIAs powered by 870hp Bristol Mercury XX and XXX engines. The squadrons which carried out this important task were 138 and 161 Squadrons, the so-called 'Moon Squadrons', both based at RAF Tempsford in Bedfordshire.

The Lysanders, or Lizzies as they were nicknamed, were painted in a matt black to keep them as inconspicuous as possible. However, it was discovered that on a moonlit night, which was when these covert flights usually took place, an aeroplane flying above a Lysander could easily spot the little aeroplane, silhouetted against the ground. Following this discovery the upper part of the fuselage and the top surface of the wings were painted in camouflage colours with just the bottom section remaining matt black.

Since the time that the aeroplane was on the ground had to be kept to a minimum, a ladder was fixed to the port side to enable agents to get in and out very quickly. On a double operation where there were agents being brought in and others taken out, one incoming agent would remain in the aeroplane to throw out baggage and to store incoming baggage, before jumping to the ground himself to make way for the homeward-bound passengers. Sometimes there was only one passenger, but on other occasions as many as four people have been known to squash into the tiny passenger space. If all went well a Lysander could be in and out of the landing ground in a matter of a few minutes, thus minimizing the risk of discovery. The Lysander brought approximately 259 agents into France and took out 431 in the years 1941–1944. This outbound number included not only agents but also political figures and others who would have been in grave danger had they remained in France.

The Lysander was not the only aeroplane used in this covert role but was probably the best known. Other aircraft used to transport both agents and supplies were the Armstrong Whitworth Whitley, Consolidated B-24 Liberator, Douglas C47, Douglas Havoc, Handley Page Halifax, Lockheed Hudson (which also picked up passengers from France), Lockheed Ventura and the Short Stirling, although not all these aircraft types were used by 138 and 161 Squadrons.

As the war progressed and more and more agents were being transported to and from France, it was decided to appoint an Air Movements Officer who could look after the details of the flights and arrange landing grounds. The person chosen for this task was a former French airline pilot, Henri Alfred Eugène Déricourt, who, in spite of successfully arranging at least fifteen flights, was ultimately discovered to be a double agent. After the war he was tried by the French courts and found not guilty. However, information received in the years since the end of the Second World War seems to confirm that he was in the employ of the Germans. He survived for many more years than most of the agents he betrayed, being killed in a plane crash in Laos on 20 November 1962.

While she was going through her parachute training at the school at Ringway in the north of England, Violette was introduced to a young Frenchman who, although he had worked in the field before, had never learned how to parachute and was attempting his training for the first time.

Major Geoffrey Mark Staunton was the assumed name of Philippe Liewer, who was the co-founder, with Canadian

Lieutenant Joseph Christian Gabriel Chartrand, of the Salesman circuit in the Rouen area of north-west France.

Born on 10 March 1911 in Paris, Philippe Liewer was educated at the Lycée Janson de Sailly and the Ecole Libre des Sciences Politique. He married fellow Parisian, Marie-Louise Weill-Halle, and the couple settled in Antibes in the south of France, where Philippe became a journalist. He spent his military service with the French army, which he left in December 1939, becoming in January 1940 a liaison officer with the British Expeditionary Force in France.

In Nice, in the summer of 1941, Liewer was introduced by a mutual friend, Mme Lambert of St Raphael, to Captain George Langelaan, who recruited him for SOE on 20 September 1941 to act as his assistant. Liewer's task was to research and report on the political feelings of the population of occupied France. However, he had been at work for only two weeks when, on 6 October 1941, the Vichy police arrested Langelaan. Unfortunately for Liewer, the police found a notebook on Langelaan in which he had written Liewer's name and address and five days later he too was arrested at his home in Antibes. The pair were sent to the Béyleme prison in Périgueux, which was a particularly nasty place plagued by vermin of all kinds and where good hygiene was non-existent and the food was terrible. They were later moved to the Vichy camp of Mauzac in the Dordogne, from where they, and a number of other agents including Robert Lyon, J.B. Hayes and Michael Trotobas, managed to escape on 16 July 1942. These escapees, along with Philippe Liewer, were all ultimately to head successful circuits, although not all would survive the war.

Following the escape, Liewer and Trotobas headed for Spain. By the end of August they had reached the Pyrenees and, having successfully crossed them, arrived in Barcelona on 1 September from where they went on to Portugal. They eventually reached London on 17 September 1942. Once in England, Liewer dropped out of sight for a few weeks. He had been sent to Scotland to recover from his ordeal and spent four weeks in the company of Aonghais Fyffe, who described him as a very pleasant young man. However, his imprisonment had taken its toll on him and he was in a bad state when he arrived. In the peace of the Scottish

Highlands he began to recover and at the end of the four weeks was well enough to return to England, where he was trained in all aspects of undercover work, was given the code name *Clement* and volunteered to return to France.

In April 1943 Liewer and Lieutenant Chartrand, code name *Dieudonné,* were flown to Pocé-sur-Cisse near Amboise in a Lysander, piloted by Flying Officer J.A. McCairns of 161 Squadron, with instructions to go to Rouen and Le Havre and set up the circuit, which became known as Salesman. On their arrival Henri Déricourt, the Air Movements Officer, received them. As the aeroplane taxied to a stop it hit a tree. The pilot blamed Déricourt for putting a light too close to the tree, as he was misled into thinking he had enough space to taxi. Déricourt blamed the pilot for not putting on his landing lights, but it would appear that Flying Officer McCairns was vindicated. When Déricourt returned to London for training he also received a reprimand for 'having endangered a Lysander through an ill-placed flare path'.

In spite of the bad start, the Salesman circuit began to take shape. Contacts with Rouen were made through the owner of a Paris dress shop, Mme Micheline. She also had a branch in Rouen, which was managed for her by Jean Sueur, who became a key figure in helping establish the circuit. It expanded rapidly and soon had many members. Liewer found accommodation for himself with a family named Francheter at 7 Place des Emmures in Rouen. He remained there for nine months until 5 February 1944 when he returned to England once more.

On 19 July Captain Isidore Newman, code name both *Pepe* and *Pierre*, arrived to be Liewer's wireless operator. He went to stay with Mme Denis Desvaux at 12 rue Jeanne d'Arc, Rouen, where he remained until March 1944. Mme Desvaux was a dressmaker and Captain Newman pretended to be her nephew. His cover story was that he had come to Rouen to help with her business. In the time up to his arrest he managed to set up several locations from which he could send his messages, fifty-four in total, often having to travel as much as forty miles between each location.

After a few weeks Chartrand transferred to the Butler circuit and was replaced by Lieutenant Robert Maloubier, code name *Paco*, who was also known as Robert Mortier, and came as an arms instructor to the Rouen circuit and assistant to Liewer. He soon became a prominent figure there.

Twenty-year-old Maloubier was fervently opposed to the Vichy government. After the fall of France he determined to escape from France and had gone to Marseilles from where he took a boat to North Africa.

In 1942 Admiral Jean François Darlan was High Commissioner in French North Africa and head of Marshal Pétain's armed forces. At the beginning of November the Allied forces mounted an operation called Operation Torch, in which they landed vast numbers of men on the shores of Algeria and Morocco. Admiral Darlan agreed to a ceasefire between the Allies and the Vichy forces on condition that he be allowed to head a liberated French government. Although the Allies supported de Gaulle and expected him to take control once France had been liberated, expediency won and they agreed to Darlan's terms. Disgusted with this turn of events, a group of young French Gaullists plotted the downfall of Darlan. In December they drew lots to elect Darlan's executioner. The task fell to twenty-year-old Fernand Bonnier de la Chapelle, who was a friend of Bob Maloubier. On Christmas Eve 1942 he managed to get into Admiral Darlan's quarters where he shot him. He must have known when he entered the premises that he had very little chance of escape and, as soon as he fired the shot that killed Darlan, he was apprehended.

Bonnier de la Chapelle was tried for his crime on Christmas Day and, on Boxing Day, was executed. In 1945 an appeals court in Paris decided that Bonnier de la Chapelle was, after all, a patriot and had acted for the good of France when he killed Admiral Darlan. In his memoirs Charles de Gaulle said that Bonnier de la Chapelle was a patriot who had acted on his own initiative. However, towards the end of the 1950s he suddenly declared that the assassination had been the work of the Americans. In an interview with an American journalist he voiced the opinion that an American diplomat, Robert Murphy, had arranged for Darlan to be shot and had then ensured that Bonnier de la Chapelle be tried, found guilty and executed before he could talk about what he had done. De Gaulle never provided any corroboration for this incredible accusation. It was known that he disliked Robert Murphy and the accusation may have been an attempt to discredit him. It was a shame that he did so by calling into question the motives of a brave and patriotic young man who had given his life for his country.

After Darlan's assassination Bob Maloubier knew that the time had come to actively join the Allies and he offered his services to them in Algiers, from where he was sent to Gibraltar and onwards to London where he was given a commission in the Army and was sent to be trained as an arms and explosives expert for SOE.

By the time that Maloubier arrived in Rouen the Salesman circuit boasted forty men in Le Havre under Roger Mayer, code name *Jean Pierre*, and eighty in Rouen under Claude Malraux, code name *Cicero*. Claude was the brother of the French novelist André Malraux, himself a leader of the Francs-Tireurs et Partisans or FTP, the communist resistance group, and future Minister of Cultural Affairs under Charles de Gaulle. He was also a Nobel Prize winner.

Maloubier parachuted into France to be met by a reception committee of half a dozen men, which included Liewer. He stayed the first night at a farm belonging to a member of the circuit and went on to Rouen the following day where he moved into a cottage belonging to a Rouen café owner. This arrangement came to an abrupt end when the owner was arrested three days later for black market activities and was held for four or five months, by which time the Germans decided he didn't have a case to answer. He may not have been a black marketeer, but if they had been a little more thorough in their investigations they would have found that, not only had he provided accommodation for Maloubier, he had also been responsible for sheltering several escaping Allied airmen. From that day Maloubier moved around the countryside instructing groups of resistance fighters and never staying in one place for very long. He posed as a publicity agent, R. Mollier, from Marseilles, who was travelling regularly between Rouen and Paris.

The main part of the circuit was divided into small groups. One person in each group knew only one person in another, thus ensuring the maximum security while providing a means of keeping in touch. Maloubier travelled between these groups by bicycle, instructing them on sabotage techniques and the use of weapons. He would usually hold his classes in the open air or in a safe house. It was not possible to have any shooting practice as this would have alerted the authorities, but resisters were taught how to use Sten guns and pistols and how to strip them down, clean and reassemble them. There were also classes in the use of explosives. A garage in Rouen was used as an explosives and arms depot with another similar facility located in the basement of a factory belonging to a member of the organization.

In addition to training members of the circuit and the local maquis, Maloubier also participated in two operations, one of which he organized himself. The first was an attack on the factory of the Cie des Metaux at Deville-les-Rouen, in which Maloubier, Claude Malraux and five others planned to blow up an electric motor and twelve pumps.

The group met at the garage used as their arms dump to fetch the explosives and their guns and then cycled to the factory. On arrival they banged on the door and tried to get the concierge to open it, but she would not do so until Malraux shouted to her in German, saying that they were policemen and that she should open the door immediately. She did so and was held up by one of the group waving a Sten gun. They all trooped into the factory with their bicycles and one remained to guard the concierge while the others went on to the guardroom. There they held up the guards and then locked them in the guardroom, leaving another of their number to watch over them while the rest went into the factory. They found two stokers and told them to leave at once, as they were about to blow up the building. The stokers thought it was an elaborate joke and laughed at the masks worn by the group. However, once they realized it was not a joke, they insisted on helping and so two more of the group were left behind, one to wait by the telephone and the other to guard the factory entrance, while the remaining three, with the two stokers, spent the next hour placing explosive charges on the twelve pumps and the electric motor. By this time the factory workers were beginning to arrive for another day's work. The man at the entrance let them in and then, at gunpoint, shut them in the guardroom with the others. About fourteen men were dealt with in this way and then the stokers were locked in the guardroom with the others who were warned that the factory was about to be blown up and that they would be safe if they just stayed where they were. Their final task was to set ten-minute time pencils, and then they retrieved their bicycles and went home. The factory was put out of action for three months after the blast and, when it resumed production, its output was seriously affected.

The operation which Maloubier organized himself was against a power station in Rouen. It was overlooked by a cliff and for some time he had watched with binoculars the gendarmes who were guarding it, learning both their habits and the layout of the power station from the safety of the cliff top. He found that there were four guards, only one of whom was continually guarding the transformers; the others usually remained in the guardroom outside the factory wall. Through London, it had been arranged for there to be an RAF raid on another part of the town to act as a diversion, but something went wrong and the British aircraft never arrived. However, the charges had been prepared and the saboteurs were ready to carry out their task and so it was decided to go ahead anyway, without the help of the RAF. One of the group went to the guardroom and captured the gendarmes, taking them off to a hut along the cliff, where they were locked up. The others held up the gendarme who was guarding the transformers with pistols and Sten guns and took him to join his comrades along the cliff. Then they went back, placed charges on the two transformers and the four switches and quickly left. They had already arrived home before the first explosion was heard!

There were other occasions when the RAF was supposed to act as a diversion, but these also did not work out. One in particular annoyed Maloubier as it was against another large power station and the group made three attempts to blow it up, but had to abandon their attempts when the RAF did not appear. This was not his only complaint against the RAF and London. He expressed his frustration at the way in which supplies were dropped, saying that they were never sent what they had asked for and that it seemed as if London sent them anything they wanted to get rid of. In spite of his complaints he was, however, of the opinion that, 'It was a bloody good organization!'

One night in December 1943 Bob Maloubier was travelling by motorcycle along a road leading out of Rouen when a *Feldgendarmerie* car flagged him down. He was not too worried as he knew his papers were all in order. He stopped, but his pillion passenger, a fellow resistance worker, did not want to take a chance and immediately leapt off the bike and escaped. The Germans wanted to know who he was and Maloubier told them he was just someone who had hitched a ride. But they didn't believe him and told him he would have to accompany them to the *Feldgendarmerie* headquarters in Oissel. The Germans didn't have anyone that evening who could ride a motorbike and so Maloubier was instructed to drive to the headquarters with a gendarme as pillion passenger, sticking a gun in his back. As they approached the headquarters building, Maloubier slowed to a stop outside the *Mairie* next door. The German car went past and also stopped. Then Maloubier jumped off his bike, knocking his passenger to the ground and pinning him underneath the overturned bike. He thinks the fall probably broke the gendarme's legs. He himself turned and ran, hotly pursued by Germans firing at him. Before long one of the bullets found its mark and he was hit in the back. Somehow he managed to keep going and eventually shook them off and returned to Rouen on foot, where he received medical attention from a sympathetic doctor.

But the prognosis was not good. The doctor believed that he would not survive and his friends realized that they would have a problem disposing of his body if he did die. They had already discovered that the Germans had contacted a number of doctors to enquire if any of them had treated a man with a gunshot wound to his back. They had probably not taken their enquiries any further at that stage as they expected a body to turn up in the near future. Not knowing what else to do, the friends obtained a sack in which to place Maloubier's body and arranged for a lorry driver to collect it and tip it into the river. However, he refused to die. Slowly he gained a little strength and, against all the odds, began to recover. The lorry driver was annoyed when, each time he came to collect the body, he found that there wasn't one. He was eventually relieved of his grizzly task altogether when it became clear that Maloubier had no intention of dying and plans were made to take him back to London where he could have a chance of a full recovery away from prying German eyes.

The weather during the early part of 1944 was particularly bad and it was not until the night of 4–5 February that an aeroplane could be sent to pick up anyone from France. The flight was originally planned to take back to London Henri Déricourt, who was by now suspected of treachery, and at the same time return some agents to England, including Philippe Liewer and Bob Maloubier. The aeroplane, a Lockheed Hudson of 161 Squadron, piloted by Squadron Leader Len Ratcliff, commander of C flight, arrived with one passenger, Gerry Morel, F Section's operations officer. He had instructions to bring back Déricourt, regardless of his objections, but when Déricourt refused, promising to return by Lysander the following week, he judged it better to allow him to do as he wished, rather than alert the Germans to the fact that he had been uncovered as a double agent and thus endanger other loyal agents working alongside him. The Hudson returned from the landing ground at Soucelles to the north-east of Angers carrying, in addition to Liewer and Maloubier, five other agents, including Robert Benoist, code name *Lionel*, whose wireless operator, Denise Bloch, was later to cross the path of Violette Szabo.

Back in London it was decided that Liewer should attend a parachute course, as it was becoming increasingly difficult and time-consuming to travel back and forward to suitable Lysander landing grounds. It was while he was attending this course at Ringway that Liewer met the girl who was to become his courier.

Chapter Seven

Into France

Soon after Philippe Liewer returned to London several members of the Salesman circuit were arrested. It was thought that the leader of the group at Serquigny, a village to the south-west of Rouen, might have been suspected of black market activities. He was arrested by the Germans on 15 February and may have told them the names of Claude Malraux and Isidore Newman. It was imperative to discover the extent of the arrests and so it was decided that Liewer, with Violette acting as his courier, would be sent to find out what had happened and to see if anything could be done to save the circuit, which was of vital importance for the D-Day plans.

The flight was arranged for the March moon period, but shortly before they were due to leave a message was received in London. It came from a circuit, code named Author, many miles away in the Corrèze. This circuit was run by Harry Peulevé, code name *Jean*, and included the FTP group under the control of Andrć Malraux, brother of Claude Malraux. The meaning of the message, although it was received in a garbled form, was quite clear. It said:

TOR 1028   12TH MARCH 1944
BLUFF CHECK OMITTED   TRUE CHECK OMITTED

73 SEVEN THREE STOP
FOLLOWING NEWS FROM ROUEN STOP XLAUDEMALRAUX DISAPPEARED BELGIVED ARRESTED BY GESTAPO STOP RADIO

OPERATOR PIERRE ARRESTES STOP IF CLETENT STILL WITH YOU DO NOT SEND HEM STOP DOFTOR ARRESTES STOP EIGHTEEN TONS ARMS REMOVED BS POLIFE STOP BELIEVE THIS DUE ARRESTATION OF A SEFTION FHEIF WHO GAVE ASRESSES ADIEU

This, of course, meant that the trip to France had to be postponed until it could be decided what was the best course of action. Liewer wanted to go directly to Rouen to find out exactly what had happened, but was eventually convinced that this would be foolhardy. Having set up the circuit nearly a year before, he was too well known to investigate the trouble himself. It was decided that Violette would go to Rouen and to Le Havre and find out whether or not the circuit was still viable and that Liewer would do what he could to ensure the safety of any of the group still at large.

The trip was set for the next moon period at the beginning of April. This allowed Violette to go to Mill Hill and spend more time with Tania. Her daughter was growing up fast and seemed to change every time she saw her. She was now almost two years old and was beginning to notice everything about her. Violette enjoyed taking care of her and playing with her. Tania, herself, has only two memories of a pretty lady she believes was her mother. In the first she was sitting up in her pram and was being taken for a walk by this pretty lady, who talked to her and smiled at her a lot. It was a fine breezy day and she could see the clouds and the blue sky. Then the weather changed and it became dull. The pretty lady put up the hood on the pram and attached the pram's apron to it and suddenly Tania could see neither the sky nor the pretty lady any more and she began to cry. She also has memories of her mother on what she believes was the last time they were ever together. Tania and her grandmother had gone out and were standing in the entrance to a building close to their home in Burnley Road. Tania sensed that something important was happening as they were saying goodbye to a lady who was dressed in dark clothes. As they said goodbye the lady disappeared into a dark hole. Tania later realized that she and her grandmother had been standing at the underground station and that the lady, Violette, had seemed to disappear into the dark hole because she had walked down the steps at the station to catch a train at the start of her second mission to France.

* * *

During this unexpected break from her duties Violette visited her parents and also spent more time with Liewer, getting to know him better. By now she had also met Bob Maloubier and had formed a firm friendship with him, taking him to meet her family. While she was waiting to go to France they exchanged friendly letters and on 11 March Violette sent him a letter in which she thanked him for his long letters and begged his forgiveness for taking so long to reply. She told him that if he would let her know when he was going to be in London she could tell him where he would be able to find her. She closed by hoping he was in good health and signed off 'Bon Baiser' (with love), adding a postscript that her brothers sent their best wishes.

It was while Violette was waiting to go to France on her first mission that she was introduced to SOE code master Leo Marks.

All agents were trained to code and decode messages. This was mostly covered at the finishing school in Hampshire, but there were also refresher courses, which were held in London. Since these were usually only for agents who would need them most, wireless operators for example, it had not been planned to give Violette a refresher course. However, the delay in going to France gave her an opportunity to become a little more proficient in this skill and it was arranged that she should go through a refresher and then receive a final briefing from Leo Marks himself.

On the appointed day Violette arrived at the SOE office at Orchard Court and was introduced to Leo Marks. He was enchanted by her and held out a secret hope that the briefing session would last all day. In his excellent book *Between Silk and Cyanide* Marks describes Violette as being, 'A dark-haired slip of mischief' and goes on to say that, 'She had a cockney accent, which added to her impishness'.

Agents were taught to code messages using a poem, unique to each individual agent, as well as to code using what was known as a WOK (worked-out key). Violette did not have any problems using the WOK but every time she tried to code or decode using her own poem she made mistakes and was unable to read back any of the messages she had encoded. It did not take Marks long to realize that Violette's poem was the cause of her problems. It was a French version of an old nursery rhyme and she obviously knew it very well. What she had not done was spell some of the words within it correctly. The poem coding system, and indeed any coding system, would only work if each word were correctly copied. It would seem that Violette had known the nursery rhyme by heart from before she could read and had probably never spelt some of the words correctly. Try as she might she just could not get her poem to work and made countless mistakes. Marks could see that she was not stupid and that she obviously had the ability to work through this problem and so he suggested that she might like to replace the nursery rhyme with another poem.

Leo Marks had had a girlfriend called Ruth whom he loved very much and wanted to marry. In December 1943 she had left England to return to Canada where she was training at an air-ambulance base. On Christmas Eve he was contacted by Ruth's father who had news that drove him to the edge of despair – Ruth had been killed in a plane crash in Canada. Not knowing what to do and wishing he had told her things that would now remain forever unsaid, he went up to the roof of Norgeby House, another of SOE's premises in Baker Street, and wrote a poem for her. It said:

The life that I have
Is all that I have
And the life that I have
Is yours

The love that I have
Of the life that I have
Is yours and yours and yours

A sleep I shall have
A rest I shall have
Yet death will be but a pause

For the peace of my years
In the long green grass
Will be yours and yours and yours.

It was to become one of the most famous poems of the Second World War, when Leo Marks decided to give the poem he had written for his lost love to Violette to use as her code poem. He didn't tell her its origin. When she asked him who had written it he merely told her he would find out and let her know when she returned from France. (See Appendix F)

Marks' generosity worked well for Violette. She loved the poem and learnt it in only a few minutes. She then went on to both code and decode a message, which was done in record time and without a single fault. The following day Violette again visited Marks at Orchard Court, this time to give him a present she told him she had won at a shooting gallery. It was a miniature chess set, which he accepted and put with some other possessions he regarded as treasures. He told her that he hoped they would be able to have a game of chess together when she returned and she laughingly told him that the time in between would allow her to learn how to play. As Marks said goodbye to her that day he knew in his heart that they would not play chess together and that he would never see her again.

Gradually the time passed. Violette must have wondered during those last few weeks before she went to France whether or not she would come back. She tried to keep busy to take her mind off the things she was about to do. She visited friends, went to the cinema, saw her parents and, of course, spent more time with Tania. She also made sure that she had made proper provision for Tania, should anything go wrong in France. She had made a will, dated 24 January 1944, and witnessed by Vera Atkins and Major R.A. Bourne Paterson who gave his address as 93 Chesterfield House, W1. Vera Atkins' address, written in her own cramped handwriting, was indecipherable. The will itself seems to have been written by Violette on a standard form, available from stationery shops, and says:

> This is the last Will and Testament of me Violette Reine Elizabeth Szabo of 36 Pembridge Villas Notting Hill W11 in the county of London made this Twenty-fourth day of January in the year of our Lord one thousand nine hundred and Forty-Four.

I HEREBY revoke all Wills made by me at any time heretofore. I appoint Reine Blanche Bushell 18 Burnley Road Stockwell SW9 to be my executor, and direct that all my Debts and Funeral Expenses shall be paid as soon as conveniently may be after my decease.
I GIVE AND BEQUEATH unto
My daughter Tania Damaris Désirée Szabo,
59 Fernside Avenue Mill Hill Edgware N7
All of which I die possessed.

V. Szabo

The will remained at the SOE offices in Miss Atkins' care until December 1945, just before SOE was wound up, when it was sent to the National Provincial Bank in Trafalgar Square for safe keeping.

The April moon period arrived and Violette went to the SOE offices to 'check in' for her flight to France. Everything that she took with her on the trip was examined. All her clothes had been made in the French style, including her shoes and handbag. Before she left for the car journey to the airfield everything she was wearing and carrying was checked to ensure there was nothing that would disclose her British nationality. The contents of her bag were taken out and the bag itself was inspected for bus tickets, cigarettes, receipts, bills and letters. Her purse contained only French money, her keys were French, her wallet housed her false papers and all the other paperwork she would need to pass as a Frenchwoman in occupied France.

She had been given the codename *Louise* and identity of Corinne Reine Leroy, the two last names being those of her mother. Her profession was shown on her identity card as a commercial secretary and her address was given as 64 rue Thiers in Le Havre. The birth date shown was her actual birthday but the place of birth was Bailleul not Levallois-Perret. With these papers it was possible for her to go to the coastal and port sectors prohibited to those not resident in the area.

When it was time to leave, Vera Atkins accompanied Violette. They were driven along the main road out of London to the north, past Edgware and Barnet, where there was a secret SOE building

1. Violette Bushell aged about 17. *(Stephen Harwood)*

2. Violette and Roy Bushell at the Savoy Hotel Ball in 1937. *(via David Earle)*

3. Albert Starmer, one of Violette Bushell's first boyfriends, on his eighteenth birthday. *(Bett Bailey)*

4. Violette in happy mood. *(via Val Weir)*

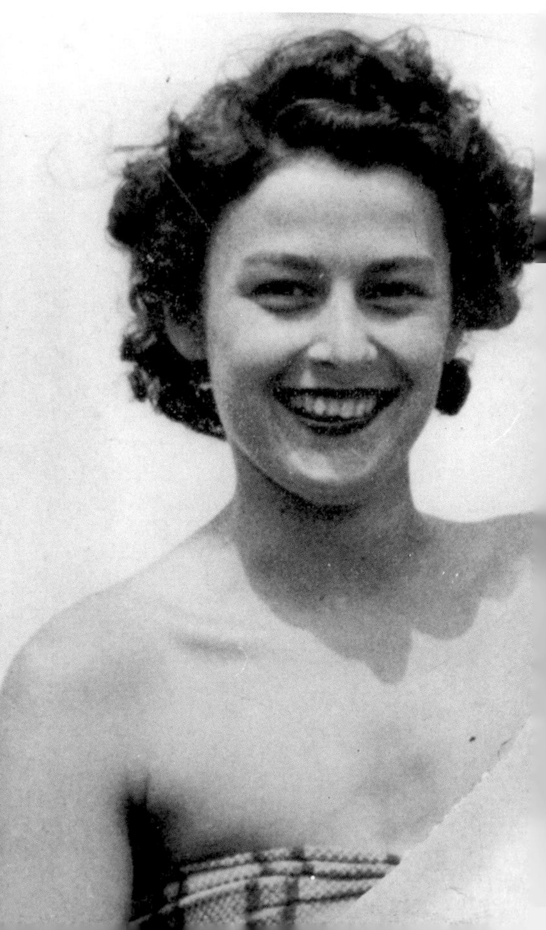

5. The wedding of Violette Bushell and Etienne Szabo at Aldershot registry office on 21 August 1940. Charles Bushell (holding coat), his wife Reine, Roy Bushell (back row), Etienne, Violette and, far right, best man Etienne Kiss. *(Roy Bushell)*

6. Violette and Etienne Szabo in the grounds of their honeymoon hotel in August 1940. *(via David Earle)*

7. A rare photo of Violette Szabo with her daughter Tania. *(via David Earle)*

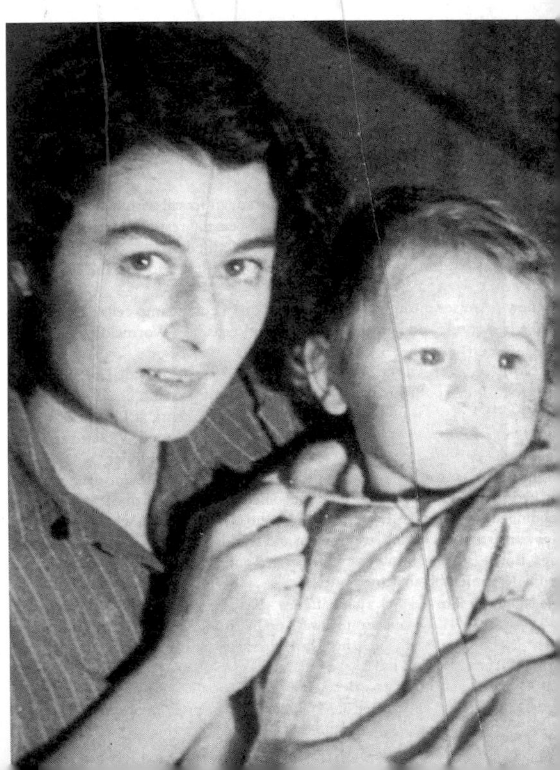

8. Georges Clement who suggested that Violette Szabo be recruited by SOE. *(SOE Advisor)*

9. Lieutenant Bob Maloubier, DSO, MC. *(SOE Advisor)*

10. Denise Bloch. *(SOE Advisor)*

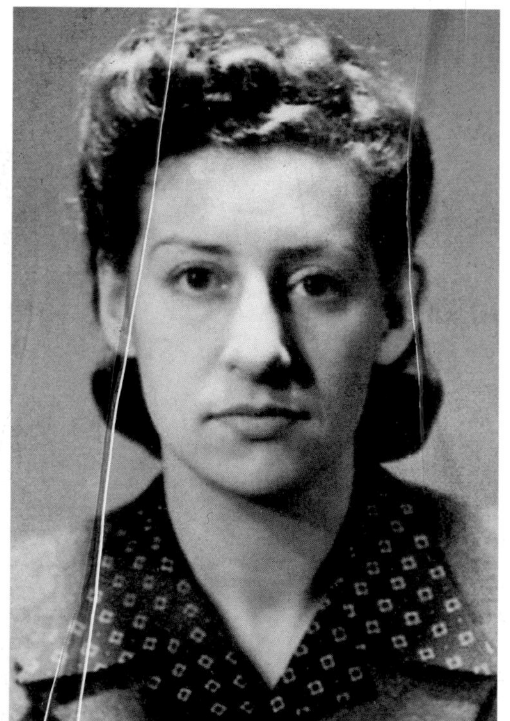

11. Lilian Rolfe. *(SOE Advisor)*

12. 36 Pembridge Villas, Notting Hill, where Violette lived between 1942 and 1944. *(Peter Bond)*

13. Winterfold in the village of Cranleigh, Surrey, where Violette attended her first SOE training course. *(Paul McCue)*

14. Norman Lucas, Violette's cousin. *(Author)*

15. Captain John Tonkin SAS *(via Paul McCue)*

16. 2nd Lieutenant Richard Crisp SAS, who, with Tonkin, spent his last afternoon at Hassell Hall with Violette Szabo, prior to being parachuted into France. Tonkin survived the war. Crisp was caught and executed. *(via Paul McCue)*

17. Hassell Hall in Bedfordshire, close to RAF Tempsford. It was here that Violette Szabo, Philippe Liewer, Bob Maloubier and Jean Claude Guiet stayed prior to their trip to France. *(Paul McCue)*

18. The memorial plaque on the wall at Gibraltar Farm barn, Tempsford airfield. *(Paul McCue)*

19. The Liberator crew who took Violette and her companions to France on the night of 7-8 June 1944. Standing L to R, Marvin 'Mike' Fenster, Avery Yancey, Richard Warn, Richard Davis. Kneeling, L to R, J.W. 'Windy' Hall, Richard Thomas, Jack Ringlesbach, Darwin Gray. *(via Carpetbagger Aviation Museum)*

20. Consolidated B-24 Liberator of the 'Carpetbagger' squadrons at Harrington, Northamptonshire. *(via Paul McCue)*

21. The fields where Violette, Philippe Liewer, Bob Maloubier and Jean Claude Guiet landed by parachute in the early hours of 8 June 1944. *(Philip Vickers)*

22. The grocer's shop in Sussac where Violette stayed during her second mission to France. *(via David Earle)*

23. The site of the German roadblock where Violette and Jacques Dufour fought. *(via David Earle)*

24. Jean Bariaud, who was in the car with Violette and Jacques Dufour when they were stopped at the German roadblock in Salon-la-Tour. *(David Harrison)*

25. A silver compact which may have been a gift from Maurice Buckmaster. The mirror is believed to have been broken during Violette's first mission to France. *(Nick Randall)*

26. B2 radio set used by agents in the field to send and receive messages. *(Ben Nock, Worcestershire)*

27. 84 Avenue Foch, where Violette was interrogated. Her name was found on the wall of cell 45. *(Author)*

28. Execution alley at Ravensbrück concentration camp, where Violette, Denise Bloch and Lilian Rolfe were shot in January 1945. The stone which marks the site says, 'Here hundreds of women and girls were murdered by the SS with shots to the back of the neck'. *(Photo courtesy of Stephanie Irvin Gowler, Berea, Kentucky, USA.)*

29. Violette Szabo's George Cross, showing inscription on reverse. *(via Val Weir)*

30. Tania receiving the Croix de Guerre from French Ambassador René Massigli on behalf of her mother. *(via Val Weir)*

31. Violette Szabo's medals. Top row, L to R. 1939-1945 Star, George Cross, France and Germany Star. Bottom row, L to R, 1939-1945 Victory Medal, Croix de Guerre. Her rank is shown as a Lieutenant although she was actually an Ensign (equivalent to 2nd Lieutenant). *(via Val Weir)*

32. Tania wearing her parents' medals. *(via Val Weir)*

33. Tania at the age of twenty-one with her grandparents, Reine and Charles Bushell. *(via Val Weir)*

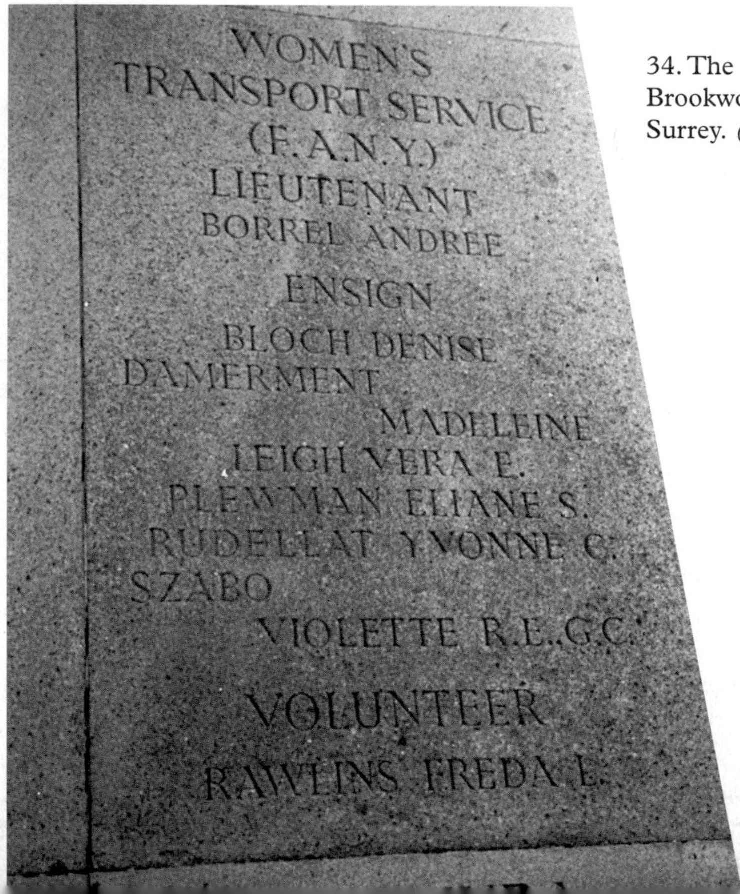

WOMEN'S
TRANSPORT SERVICE
(F.A.N.Y.)
LIEUTENANT
BORREL ANDREE
ENSIGN
BLOCH DENISE
DAMERMENT
MADELEINE
LEIGH VERA E.
PLEWMAN ELIANE S.
RUDELLAT YVONNE C.
SZABO
VIOLETTE R.E.,G.C.
VOLUNTEER
RAWLINS FREDA L.

34. The FANY Memorial at Brookwood Cemetery in Surrey. *(Paul McCue)*

35. The memorial at the site of the Neue Bremm concentration camp in Saarbrücken, where Violette Szabo was held prior to being transported to Ravensbrück. The memorial was built by workgroups of young Germans. *(Stephan Barton)*

36. The unveiling of the blue plaque outside 18, Burnley Road. *(Stephen Harwood)*

37. Left to Right: Jean Claude Guiet, Tania Szabo, Bob Maloubier and friends at the opening of the Violette Szabo museum at Wormelow in 2000. *(Author)*

38. The Violette Szabo Memorial Mural in Stockwell, June 2001. *(Nick Randall)*

in which were manufactured all kinds of gadgets for use by secret agents. They then went north, past Hatfield, home of the de Havilland aircraft company, on to Baldock and Biggleswade until they came to the small Bedfordshire town of Sandy where they left the main road and headed east to Hassell Hall, a large country house, from where the agents were taken to RAF Tempsford for their flights to France.

In his book *Specially Employed*, published in 1952, Maurice Buckmaster devotes an entire chapter to Violette and describes her as being 'really beautiful, dark-haired and olive-skinned, with that kind of porcelain clarity of face and purity of bone that one finds occasionally in the women of the south-west of France'. He tells how when he checked her cover story before she left for France, he felt that she would, 'convince even the most sceptical and incredulous member of the French *Milice*'. He recalls how her training reports described her as being ambitious, enthusiastic, very athletic, quick to pick up new ideas and having a lively intelligence. He was of the opinion that there was, 'no one more likely to carry out successfully this most hazardous task'.

There are many errors in Colonel Buckmaster's account, not least the fact that he has made Violette's two missions into one. He has also rewritten her training record in glowing terms, quite different from those actually held on her personal file. It will be remembered that her instructors were doubtful if she would make the grade at all as an agent, much less excel at it. The task of finding out what had happened to a circuit, part of which had operated in a prohibited area, was a difficult one. It is almost unbelievable that Buckmaster thought she would have no trouble convincing 'even the most sceptical and incredulous member of the French *Milice*' when all her training reports recorded that she spoke French with a marked English accent. If Colonel Buckmaster was seeking to make her out as a heroine, he was wasting his time. Violette's actions in the field did that for her without any assistance from him.

Perhaps the key to the puzzle is Violette's own motive for wanting to be an agent in the first place. She told Bob Maloubier that what she wanted more than anything was to kill Germans. At the age of twenty-two she was a widow, with a young child. She had only lived with her late husband for two weeks during their marriage and both of these weeks were in a holiday atmosphere. The first week was their honeymoon and the second, one year later, was the hurried leave spent together in Liverpool before Etienne returned to Africa, more a second honeymoon than the beginnings of married life together. As a result of this second week she had her daughter, Tania, but her husband had been taken from her and a part of her life was over for ever. She felt cheated and hurt – one of her training reports mentions her mood swings and her depression – and she was desperately in need of revenge. All she wanted was to take away the lives of those she believed had destroyed her life. This was why she was willing to put herself in danger and go to occupied France. I don't believe that she was either unknowing or uncaring of what might happen to her. She was not a stupid person and must have known the danger, but her desire for revenge was so strong that it surmounted every other emotion. Whoever countermanded the decision not to send her into the field must have realized that this single-mindedness could be useful. It is possible, even likely, that it was Colonel Buckmaster himself who made the decision to send her to France. Was his lyrical description of her beauty and extravagant claims about her abilities his way of justifying the decision to send her? Violette's courage and fortitude were not in question, but what was in doubt was her ability to protect herself against the dangers she would undoubtedly face when she was in such a delicate emotional state.

Although there were flights to France by Lysander on the night of 5 April 1944, Violette's was not one of them. She and Philippe Liewer were parachuted into enemy territory from a Consolidated B-24 Liberator bomber, which had been sent from the USAAF base at Harrington in Northamptonshire to pick them up. Harrington was the home of the Eighth Air Force's Special Operations Group and had only been in operation for about a month. The building of the airfield began in 1943 and was completed in the spring of 1944 by the 826 and 852 Engineer Battalions of the US Army. It had been intended as a Class A airfield for heavy bombers, but by March 1944 the 801st Bomber Group, under the command of Lieutenant Colonel Clifford J. Heflin, was based there with four squadrons of Liberators, the so called ‘Carpetbagger’ squadrons, for use in the assistance of the resistance forces of France, Holland, Belgium and Norway, dropping both agents and supplies. Some of the original buildings of what had been Gibraltar Farm before the airfield was built still existed. The barn had been left intact and was used to store parachutes and other equipment issued to the agents just prior to their departure. Today Gibraltar Farm barn has been converted into a small museum, detailing its use by those agents. For many of them it was the last place in England they ever saw.

Violette and Philippe Liewer were given a final check and were issued with their parachutes before climbing into the bomber. As it lumbered down the runway and lifted into the air there must have been some sense of nervousness and tension on board the aircraft. Liewer had, until this time, avoided the possibility of a parachute jump and Violette had been as nervous during her second parachute training as she had during the first. In addition they were about to jump, at night, into a country occupied by enemy forces not knowing what danger awaited them at their destination. Not to have been even a little bit nervous would surely indicate a lack of comprehension of the seriousness of their situation. But they did know that they were going to an area and to a circuit that had been severely compromised and it is extremely doubtful that they were unaware of the danger. They could not even be certain that they would be received by friendly forces and might have to make their way to Rouen without any support on the ground.

When the time came, Violette sat waiting for the signal to jump. It came and she dropped through the hole in the bottom of the aircraft fuselage feeling, moments later, the jerk on her harness as the parachute unfurled and billowed into the night air. She floated down towards the ground and, as she landed and struggled with her parachute, she became entangled with the harness and couldn’t free herself. She heard voices and didn’t dare to move, thinking that they might be Germans. Then, as they came closer, she could hear that they were French and, knowing that she was safe, she finally managed to free herself from her parachute. Quickly struggling to gather it up, she was confronted with the reception committee. Liewer had landed nearby and the two were taken to a safe house where they stayed for what remained of the night. The next day they went on to Paris from where Violette boarded a train bound for Rouen.

The train was crowded and the journey irritating. It was impossible to ignore the Germans who seemed to be everywhere one looked. Violette soon found that it was also impossible to avoid them. German soldiers, seeing a pretty young girl carrying a bag, immediately offered assistance; seats were given up, doors opened, cigarettes offered and Violette had to remember all the time not to speak too much to them in case her English accent gave her away. She also had to regard them in the way a native Frenchwoman would have done with, perhaps, weary resignation rather than the hatred that she herself felt. The *Milice*, who would never have mistaken her accent for that of a Frenchwoman, posed a greater danger to Violette. Although by early 1944 many more French people were opposed to the Vichy government than had been before, there were still those who regarded the government and its agents, such as the *Milice*, as being the true government of their country and thought of resisters as traitors. It was very difficult to know whom one could trust.

The situation that Violette found when she arrived in Rouen was not good. One of the first things she saw was a poster, showing photos, albeit rather bad ones, of both Philippe Liewer and Bob Maloubier. Liewer's picture was captioned 'Clément' while that of Maloubier gave his name as R. Mollier, his cover name as the publicity agent from Marseilles. Violette later spotted more damning posters and, when she judged it safe, managed to rip one from a wall and stuff it into her bag to be brought back to England. One wonders about the wisdom of such an action. Had she been searched at any time she would surely have been in trouble if the poster had been discovered.

For the next three weeks Violette made her way around the narrow streets of Rouen visiting houses and flats and trying to discover what had happened to the occupants. It soon became clear to her that the circuit had been thoroughly penetrated and that most of its members had been arrested. It was a delicate task trying to discover what had happened without arousing suspicion about herself.

She discovered that the Francheter family, who had provided a home for Liewer while he set up the Salesman circuit, were still free and living in their apartment at 7 Place des Emmures. Mme Desvaux, the dressmaker who had looked after Isidore Newman at 12 rue Jeanne d'Arc, had not been so lucky; her home had been bombed and she had had to move. A resister named Paccaud and another named Piontik, both of whom had been part of a sabotage group which had blown up a ship, still appeared to be free, as did the Dussaux brothers, one of whom was an informer from police headquarters and the other an informer on industrial installations. The only other people who seemed to have escaped arrest were the *Commissionaire de Police* for the 4th district of Rouen, M. Theveneau, and the *Regulateur Chef de Rouen*, M. Queneau.

The list of those who had not been so lucky was depressingly long. Violette found that most of the group from Rouen and the surrounding areas had been arrested and were thought to have been deported to Germany. These included Victor and Charles Thivenet, Henri and Raoul Boulanger, Andre Quietteville, Robert Boron, Claude Charville, Roland Lami, Rene Franconville, Henri Richard, Robert Roussel, Ernest Lizeaux, Louis Crodemer, Roger Godebout, Augustin L'Hote and Leon and Jean van Meistier. These were the men who had acted as reception committees for receiving agents and supplies and some had also been members of the sabotage groups active in the Rouen area.

Of Claude Malraux and Isidore Newman Violette found few signs. Malraux had been arrested around 25 February and Newman at the end of March. Newman's landlady, Mme Desvaux, had also been arrested, but was later released. Neither Malraux nor Newman survived the war. Following their arrests they were taken, along with other members of the Salesman circuit, to Compiègne and from there onwards into Germany. Isidore Newman was executed at Mauthausen concentration camp on 6 September 1944.

As to what had happened in Le Havre no one seemed to know. Security had been very tight there and it was impossible to find out anything about that branch of the Salesman circuit. The only fact that could be discovered was that Roger Mayer, Liewer's second in command, had been almost beaten to death by the Gestapo in an attempt to make him give them the names of other members of the circuit. Mayer had not given away a single name and, following his torture, had been sent to Germany. In the end, after speaking with Violette, Liewer came to the conclusion that they would not be able to get any details until Roger Mayer returned from Germany. He did survive his imprisonment and returned to France in 1945, although the time spent in Germany had destroyed his health. Soon after his return he was awarded the Military Cross for his bravery.

In October 1944 Liewer sent a recommendation to London that Hugues Paccaud be given a decoration for his work with the Salesman circuit in Rouen. His message says:

> With the greatest coolness he managed to take his explosive charge into a heavily guarded ship-yard and blow up and sink an enemy minesweeper despite the presence of large numbers of German officials, and this only three hours before the ship was due to leave. At a later date he took part in a very successful attack on the transformer station at Dieppedalle.

The destruction of the minesweeper, to which Liewer referred, took place in the shipyard of Ateliers et Chantiers de Normandie near Rouen in early September 1943. The attack on the power station happened on 31 October 1943 and brought it to a complete standstill for the following six months.

Having done all she could to find out what had happened to the ill-fated Salesman circuit, Violette once again boarded a train and made her way back to Paris to meet up with Philippe Liewer. It had been arranged that a Lysander would pick them up on 30 April for the return trip to England, which gave Violette exactly two days to explore the French capital.

Although she had not been there for some years, it was where she had spent the earliest days of her childhood. It was also the place that she and Etienne had planned to return to when the war was over. Now she had to walk the streets alone, knowing that she would never see them with her husband.

The Paris of Violette's childhood had been a very different place. Although the buildings, monuments and parks were still there they were now surrounded by Germans, who had taken over everything. The railways came under German control, as did other public transport. The taxis had all but disappeared to be replaced with vélo-taxis, contraptions much like the oriental rickshaw, which were pedal-powered and operated by a number of former Tour de France cyclists. The cars that did remain in the city were wood-burning *gazogènes,* equipped with huge boilers. Street signs were written in German and pointed to organizations that were now under German control. The streets were full of the sounds of wooden clogs that many Parisians wore because of the shortage of shoe leather and of German soldiers' boots against the cobbles. What was worse was to see Germans goose-stepping down the Champs Elysées.

Although there was a severe shortage of food in Paris by the spring of 1944, there were still a number of smart restaurants, such as Maxim's, where those who could afford the extortionate prices could dine well. For the less well off it was difficult even to get a portion of *pommes frites.* Singers such as Edith Piaf and dancers, Serge Lifar and Zizi Jeanmaire, provided the entertainment; nightclubs like the Moulin Rouge were filled with Germans and their French girlfriends each night and the famous Gaumont-Palace cinema was run on electricity generated by four young men pedalling like mad on bicycles. The racetracks at Auteuil and Longchamps were still operating but were frequented only by Germans and wealthy French collaborators.

Although tired after her exhausting trip to Rouen, Violette couldn't resist visiting some of the sights of Paris. She went into the shops where it was still possible to buy perfume and bought some for herself and for her mother. She found a little boutique where she managed to buy a dress for Tania. Although it was small, she knew that it would be too big, but was unable to do any better as most of the small children who would normally have been in Paris had been sent out of the city and there was no call for tiny clothes at that time.

Coming at last to the imposing columns of the Madeleine, she wearily climbed the steps and went into the building that she and Etienne had planned to visit to give thanks for their survival. Now the church, with its beautiful painted domes and coloured marble, was a place of pilgrimage rather than thanksgiving, as she prayed for the soul of her dead husband. Emerging into the daylight again she found herself at the top of the steps, looking down the elegant rue Royale towards the Place de la Concorde. On a whim she walked down the street until, at the bottom on the right-hand side, she came upon the premises of the couturier Molyneux at number 5. Gazing at the lovely dresses, her fondness for beautiful clothes was just too much for her and she went inside and placed an order. When they learnt of this back at SOE in London, those who had wondered whether or not Violette might have been suicidal following Etienne's death must surely have had their answer. A woman with thoughts of suicide might perhaps buy one beautiful dress to wear before her death. Violette, however, purchased three dresses and added to that total a smart jumper, described as a yellow golf jersey!

While I was trying to find out more about the clothes that Violette bought, I was in touch with Peter Hope Lumley, who is the nephew of designer Edward Molyneux. He wrote me a charming letter in which he told me:

> In 1944 and, indeed, since the fall of Paris, Molyneux was in German hands, Edward Molyneux having fled to London, leaving his business in the hands of some of his staff, who ran the house and, indeed, were able to give it back to him virtually intact at the end of the war. Therefore – an ironic twist – Mrs Szabo actually bought her garments from the Germans!

Violette's dresses were purchased at a total cost of 37,475 francs including tax, which, at the exchange rate of the time, amounted to about £213, in those days a huge amount to spend on three dresses and a sweater, especially for Violette who had never had very much money. They were, however, beautiful dresses, one in black crepe, another in red tartan and the third in a floral print. There were minor alterations to be made and on the morning that she was due to return to England Violette went, once again, to the rue Royale to fetch her purchases. As she went in and out of the shops, looking for last-minute gifts, she saw a pair of pretty red floral earrings that she bought for herself. Then, with her shopping firmly packed into her baggage, she and Liewer made their way to a small field south-west of Châteauroux to await the Lysanders that were to take them home.

The aeroplanes arrived within minutes of each other and they quickly climbed aboard. Flying Officer J.P. Alcock, on his first operational flight, took Liewer home and Violette travelled with Flight Lieutenant R. Large, both of 161 Squadron. Of course the two aircraft had not been sent to France only to fetch Liewer and Violette. On this trip they had also brought out three more agents in a joint operation codenamed Organist.

The operational instructions for Organist, dated 27 April 1944, expected there to be four outbound passengers, not three, and a number of packages, whose weight and dimensions were still to be decided. The number of returning passengers was undecided at the time when the operational instructions were made out. The landing points for the Lysander were called Hercule and Fortune and were south-south-west of Châteauroux and west of Arthon. The wind direction was the determining factor as to which end of the field the aeroplane landed. Hercule was the designated area for this particular flight and was slightly closer to Châteauroux, but there were special instructions which noted, 'Flare path to be laid on Fortune if wind direction unsuitable for Hercule.' The flare path to guide the Lysander in was to be laid out by someone on the ground who was known as Olive and had been trained under the name of Lieutenant Shaw. The operational report described Lieutenant Shaw as being, 'quite an intelligent officer. His work was satisfactory and he should make a good operator. Acted as assistant to Regis X on operation Chauffeur, April moon. Speaks fair English.' The reception committee was due to stand by at the field between 22.30 hours and 01.30 hours to receive the aircraft and this, of course, meant that Violette and Liewer had to be there between those times as they only had a few minutes for the inbound passengers to deplane before they had to be on board and ready to depart. The other vital piece of information given in the instructions was the recognition letters. These were the codes flashed between the aircraft and the reception committee and told both the pilot and those on the ground that everything was all right to land. These codes were designed to guard against the possibility of the Germans receiving a flight and arresting whoever came in with the aircraft. The recognition letters for Operation Organist were to be AD and BN, the former being sent air to ground and the latter ground to air.

Tragically this was to be the first and last successful operation for Flying Officer Alcock. On his next Lysander flight he was shot down by an RAF De Havilland Mosquito whose pilot mistook the aircraft for a Luftwaffe Fieseler Storch.

In *Carve Her Name with Pride* R.J. Minney has described Violette's flight home as being, 'smooth and without incident'. In reality it was the exact opposite. The aeroplane that Flight Lieutenant Large was flying that night was JR-N V9490. On the homeward journey they flew very close to the airfield at Châteaudun. Suddenly out of nowhere there were searchlights sweeping the night sky and enemy fighters ready to do great damage to the small, relatively slow Lysander. The only means of communication between the pilot and his passenger was by an intercom, which could be switched off by the pilot. As soon as it became obvious to Bob Large that he was a little too close to Châteaudun because he was being fired upon, he turned off the intercom so that he could concentrate on getting them out of trouble. He knew he would have a difficult job doing so. Just before he had silenced the intercom he had heard Violette screeching into it. She must have been terrified by the unexpected experience of being shot at and seeing flak bursting all around them. Knowing that he would not be able to cope with an hysterical woman and fly the plane at the same time, he thought he would leave the intercom switched off until they were out of danger. By a series of manoeuvres Bob eventually got the aeroplane out of the danger zone. He had to fling the Lysander around the sky to do so and realized that the woman in the back (he didn't know her name at that time) had been thrown around rather a lot.

As soon as they were back on a straight and level course Bob had intended to switch the intercom back on. However, once they were back to relative safety, he forgot and it never occurred to him how quiet his passenger had been during the rest of the journey. As he made a landing approach at RAF Tempsford he was not aware that the drama was not yet over. A Lysander has a fixed undercarriage and, while they were being shot at near to Châteaudun, one of the tyres had been hit and was now in shreds. The aeroplane touched down to a very bumpy landing and ground-looped. Again Violette was flung about in her seat. When he finally managed to bring the Lysander to a stop, Bob jumped down and went to rescue his passenger. He was greeted with an angry tirade in rapid French, unfairly he thought at the time. He had, after all, managed to get her back safely, albeit a bit bumpily. What Bob discovered later was that Violette had been flung about so much on landing that she had not seen Bob jump out of the aeroplane. When this young man confronted her, she was sure that they had crashed in enemy territory, that the pilot was dead and that he was a German come to arrest her. He was tall and blond, after all, exactly like the many German soldiers she had seen in Paris and it was too dark properly to identify his uniform. Bob's French wasn't really up to answering Violette's hail of abuse and he had no way of knowing that she also spoke English. Trying to placate her, he called up for a car to be sent to fetch them both. He said that he was very glad that Violette didn't have a gun with her, as he was sure that, had she had one, she would have shot him. Then the car arrived and the mix-up was sorted out. Suddenly a broad smile appeared on Violette's face and she exclaimed, '*Vous êtes pilote!*' Then, flinging her arms around his neck, she kissed him. As the car drove off with Violette safely on board, Bob stood for a moment by his damaged aeroplane, bemused by the events that had just taken place. Then he decided that it had been worth it all, just to get that kiss!

Chapter Eight

Salesman 2

When Violette arrived back in London she went straight to Burnley Road to see her parents and to assure them that she was safe. Then she went to the SOE offices where she met up with Philippe Liewer again. He suggested that they have dinner together that night at the Studio Club and invited Bob Maloubier to join them. Violette is said to have worn one of the Molyneux dresses and to have looked stunning.

Norman Lucas, Violette's cousin, had just got leave from his ship and was in London with his mother, Mr Bushell's sister Florence. They were staying at Burnley Road for a few days and Violette and Norman resumed their old friendship and went out to a few clubs while they had the chance. They went around London together as they had in the old days.

When I spoke to Norman about his cousin, he suddenly recalled how Violette had once shown him how to get into the London Zoo without paying by climbing through a hole in the fence! He also remembered going to a club with her one evening during the leave he spent in London. They were in a taxi when suddenly she spotted someone she knew. She stopped the taxi and got out to speak to the young man. Norman said that he realized, once he had found out what she had really done in the war, that it must have been one of her SOE colleagues. She didn't say a word about the meeting when she got back into the taxi, she just continued with the conversation she and Norman had been having before. Then they made their way to the club as they had planned and had a very pleasant evening.

When the time came for Aunt Florence and Norman to go back to Herefordshire they asked Violette to go with them. She was delighted and had a really good break away from any thoughts of the war. She and Norman found plenty to do and, although she didn't speak much about what she had been through, she did tell him something of what she had been doing. He told me that he thinks she felt able to do so, not only because she trusted him not to say anything, but also because, being in the Navy, he too was bound by the terms of the Official Secrets Act.

During her stay at Wormelow Violette took her young cousins, John and Brenda, to the May Fair, which was held every year in the streets of Hereford. She was wearing the red earrings that she had bought for herself in Paris and, unfortunately, at one point tripped and one of the earrings came off. In spite of a search it could not be found. When Violette took the remaining earring off, she dropped it into a drawer in her bedroom at The Old Kennels and forgot about it. It remained there for some time until Aunt Florence took it and kept it safe. It was recently rediscovered and has been promised to the Violette Szabo Museum as an exhibit where it may well already be on show. (See Appendix D)

Soon it was time for Violette to return home and she and Norman took the train back to the capital together. What Violette did not know at that time was that while she was in Herefordshire plans were underway for her promotion. On 4 May F Section applied to the FANY to promote her to Ensign in recognition of her work in Rouen. The memo said that she had:

> Just returned from an important mission in the field which she has performed admirably. It is desired to recognize this before she goes out again by commissioning her as an Ensign in the F.A.N.Y.s

On or about 25 May 1944 Violette received her commission.

On her return from Herefordshire Violette had gone back to her flat in Notting Hill. She now had nothing to do until F Section came up with her next task. She kept in touch with her friends as before and often entertained them at the flat. Bob Maloubier was a frequent visitor. They used to play records together and one particular favourite was a recording of the Mills Brothers singing *I'll Be Around.* Bob recalled that it became their theme tune and they often sang it themselves when they were together. He told me that Violette was always either singing or humming little tunes to herself.

Time now hung heavy for Violette. She sometimes went to Mill Hill to visit Tania and on one or two occasions took the little girl to the SOE offices to meet her colleagues and be shown off to them all. Lieutenant Gordon Nornable, who worked alongside Colonel Richard Heslop, code name *Xavier*, in the Marksman circuit, remembers seeing Violette with Tania at the SOE office in Wimpole Street during this period. Yvonne Baseden, code name *Odette*, the wireless operator with the Scholar circuit and later fellow prisoner at Ravensbrück, also remembers seeing Violette with her daughter. She was surprised that Violette had brought the child to the office, as she had not seen any of the other agents' children there before.

In May 1944 the leader of the Stationer circuit, Maurice Southgate, code name *Hector*, was arrested. Stationer was a huge circuit covering a vast area from Châteauroux in Indre down as far as Tarbes and Pau in the foothills of the Pyrenees.

Southgate's career had been fraught with danger even before joining SOE. He had been on the *Lancastria*, the ill-fated ship which left the port of St Nazaire on 17 June 1940 and was bombed by the Germans and sank. Nearly 3000 troops and civilians were drowned. Southgate was lucky to have escaped. He came to SOE from the RAF as a Squadron Leader in 1942 when he was twenty-nine years old. Although British by nationality, he had been born in Paris and was brought up there. One of his childhood friends had been John Starr, code name *Bob*, who also worked for SOE. He was to regret the friendship when, after his arrest by the Gestapo, he was taken to avenue Foch where John Starr was also being held and he was immediately recognized and greeted by name by his old school friend. John Starr identified several agents for the Germans in this way. In return for his help he was given his own room and good food, and was set to work drawing portraits of the Germans. Although eventually sent to Mauthausen, he survived the war, escaped prosecution for his treachery, although he was arrested and held for a time, and went on to live a quiet life in Paris.

Southgate had arrived in France in January 1943 when he was parachuted in with his courier Jacqueline Nearne, code name *Jacqueline*. Although Southgate came back to England for a brief period, Jacqueline Nearne remained in France until April 1944 when she was eventually brought out by a Lysander, piloted by Flight Lieutenant Taylor, on the night of 9–10 April. She later appeared in a film about SOE made during the war but not released until 1946. It was called *Now It Can Be Told* and also starred another real life agent, Harry Rée, code name *César*.

Southgate was arrested when he went to visit one of the Stationer wireless operators in Montluçon. Although he had always stressed to the circuit members the importance of good security, he was let down by a momentary lapse when he failed to see the danger signal left for him by the wireless operator. Oblivious to the danger ahead of him, he walked straight into the house and was immediately arrested by the Gestapo. Following his betrayal by John Starr in the avenue Foch, Southgate was taken to Buchenwald, from where he was safely released at the end of the war.

After his arrest Stationer was divided into two more manageable groups. In the northern part of the circuit the areas around Châteauroux, Valençay and Issoudun were taken over by a courier who had come to SOE from the WAAF, Pearl Witherington, code name *Marie*. This new circuit was called Wrestler. The southern part, to the south-east of Wrestler, was taken over by Amédée Maingard, code name *René*, Southgate's wireless operator, and was renamed Shipwright. This left a gap in the Haute Vienne, which SOE planned to fill with another new circuit called Salesman 2, to be run by Philippe Liewer, under his new code name, *Hamlet*. The task of this new circuit would be to liaise with both the leaders of the other circuits in the area and with the leaders of the local maquis, to ensure that there would be as much disruption to transport and lines of communication in the area as possible in support of the D-Day landings.

In the middle of May Liewer arranged a lunch party at a restaurant in Soho. He invited Violette and Bob Maloubier to meet the new member of their team, Jean Claude Guiet, a nineteen-year-old American wireless operator. Guiet had briefly met Maloubier, whom he knew as Bob Mortier, but had not met the attractive FANY officer who was introduced to him as Corinne. The conversation during lunch was general but Guiet realized that the other three knew each other well and that there was a relaxed, informal feeling between them. Guiet himself was reluctant to say much, being the newcomer to the group. Violette had made a strong impression on him. He said of her, 'She was lively, informal, full of fun. About five feet three inches, she was lithe and moved gracefully.'

Guiet was not to see anything of the other three members of his new team for about three weeks, but D-Day was fast approaching and there was work to be done. During that time he was busy with his own personal arrangements, checking his clothing, sorting out codes and reviewing his cover story. Then, on 4 June, they all met up again at RAF Tempsford. Unfortunately the team did not manage to get back to France in time for the Allied landings on the Normandy beaches. They went through all their checks, had their equipment issued to them and struggled into the clothes they would be wearing for the drop. Vera Atkins, who had accompanied Violette to the airfield, sent them off with the traditional salute, 'Merde!', and they finally climbed aboard the aeroplane ready for take off. The plane began to taxi towards the runway; then, suddenly, it stopped and they were told that the operation had been postponed due to bad weather. The feeling of anti-climax and disappointment was enormous. Having prepared themselves mentally for the task they were facing, they were all anxious that the waiting be over so that they could get on with their work. But the weather could not be controlled and so they reluctantly went back to Hassell Hall for another night.

The next day, having too much time to kill and nothing to do, they drove over to Cambridge where they had a pleasant lunch and a stroll around the city. There was a lot of laughter and joking and they sang the song that was, by now, regarded as the entire team's theme song, *I'll Be Around*. One wonders what the people of Cambridge must have thought of this strange little group; two big Frenchmen, one American and a tiny Anglo-

French girl, all singing in their various accents while wandering around the city.

The weather wasn't very pleasant that day either, low clouds and a strong wind, and so they returned to Hassell Hall in the afternoon. Violette went into the lounge and chatted to two young men, Lieutenant Richard Crisp and Captain John Tonkin, who were attempting to complete a jigsaw puzzle. Unlike many of the people at Hassell Hall, these two men were not with SOE. They were members of the SAS and were about to go to France on an operation called Bulbasket. Their task on arrival was to carry out attacks on various sites including blowing up sections of the rail system and destroying lines of communication. Crisp and Tonkin parachuted into an area near to Châteauroux from a Handley Page Halifax of 161 Squadron in the early hours of the morning of 6 June 1944. D-Day had arrived.

At the same time that Crisp and Tonkin were making their last-minute preparations, the Salesman 2 team were getting ready for France. Checks were carried out again, equipment issued, good-byes said and finally they were on another aeroplane, which, this time, did take off. They settled down to the coffee and sandwiches that had been provided for the journey and again began the mental preparation for what lay ahead. After a flight of about three hours they reached the dropping zone, but again something was wrong. This time there was no reception committee waiting for them and the aeroplane turned back for England with its precious cargo still on board. As they flew back over France and towards the English Channel the Allied forces in their landing craft were travelling in the opposite direction, beginning the invasion that would, ultimately, lead to the end of the Second World War in Europe. For the Salesman team the journey back to England was another let-down. They spent the time dozing, singing and chatting to the dispatcher. Then they were making the approach to RAF Tempsford. Before long they were all back at Hassell Hall where, exhausted by the night's non-events, they fell into their beds and went to sleep.

About three hours after getting into bed Liewer, Maloubier and Guiet were awoken by Violette with the news that the invasion of Europe had begun. At first they didn't believe her. She had acquired the reputation of being a joker and they all thought that this was another of her pranks and not a very funny one either, since they were all so tired. But Violette assured them that she was serious and that the invasion had really started. Sleep deserted them and they sat around talking about what would be happening from now on. They were angry with the crew of the aeroplane that had taken them to France for not telling them what was going on. They were convinced that the crew must have been able to see something of the vast force that was making its way across the Channel and yet not one of them had thought to tell the team. Had they known they could have watched it all through the hole in the aircraft meant for their parachute jumps.

The team spent D-Day at Hassell Hall. None of them wanted to go out; they were too keyed up to do anything except think about their trip, which they were sure would happen that night. Professor Foot in *SOE in France*, E.H. Cookridge in *Inside SOE* and R.J. Minney in *Carve Her Name With Pride* have all placed the flight on 6–7 June. However, Guiet told me that they flew out the day after D-Day, which would make it the night of the 7–8 June and this is confirmed by a report from Group Captain G.F. Wood addressed to HQ Bomber Command giving details of flights carried out by Harrington Liberators. Under the date 7–8 June is listed Operation Stationer 110B (Seamstress/Porter/Salesman/Guardian) and the name of the pilot. There were, in fact, no Harrington Liberators shown as flying on the night 6–7 June.

The day of their departure was spent playing ping-pong and cards. Violette played cards and won; she played a fairly good game of ping-pong as well. Vera Atkins, who had also stayed at the Hall, remarked on Violette's calm behaviour that last day in England.

Eventually night fell and they went to the old barn for the third time to collect their supplies. Their personal baggage contained their uniforms, which they hoped to be able to wear eventually now that the invasion was underway. Violette was humming a little tune to herself as she got ready.

They flew in a Consolidated B24-D Liberator, 42-40538K, of 36 Bomber Squadron, part of the 801st Bomber Group based at USAAF Harrington. As with Violette's first trip, the Liberator flew in to Tempsford from Harrington to pick up its passengers.

It had a crew of eight under the command of pilot, Marvin L. Fenster, who was known to his friends as Mike. The remaining crew were:

Richard A. Warn, co-pilot
Richard C. Davis, navigator
Avery W. Yancey, bombardier
J.W. 'Windy' Hall, dispatcher
John C. Ringlesbach, radio operator
Richard W. Thomas, engineer
Darwin S. Gray, gunner

The Liberator took off at 22.26 hours. Liewer, Maloubier, Guiet and Violette were all quite relaxed and ready for action. They spent the flight time playing cards. In a letter I received from Dorothy Ringlesbach, wife of John C. Ringlesbach the radio operator, she told me:

> Jack says about all he remembers of Szabo as a person is that she was of medium height and resembled pictures he has seen of her taken at that time. All the agents wore heavily padded jump suits. Before she jumped she insisted upon kissing each member of crew including pilot and co-pilot.

The weather at the dropping zone, which was in the vicinity of the village of Sussac, thirty miles to the south-east of Limoges, was fair and visibility was good, between ten and fifteen miles. Liewer jumped first. As she followed him, Violette winked at Jean Guiet. It was 01.49 hours on the morning of 8 June. Then twelve containers of supplies were pushed out through the hole in the floor of the aircraft and floated down to earth behind the two agents, landing about twenty yards away from the lights on the ground. Mike Fenster brought the giant bomber around for a second run over the dropping zone and, three minutes after their colleagues had left the Liberator, Guiet and Maloubier jumped, to be followed by all the agents' personal baggage. One of the crew observed that they all landed on target. The Liberator then came around once more for its final run when ten more packs of supplies were dropped at 01.58 hours, again on target. The aircraft then turned once more but this time headed for home. It landed safely back at base at Harrington at 05.17 hours.

A large, excited reception committee greeted the four agents. Parachutes were swiftly gathered up, baggage, boxes and packs were collected together and stacked in a lorry and the agents themselves climbed into a large black car for the short journey to the village of Sussac. Here they were taken to a grocer's shop in the village square. Food had been prepared for them and they were given rooms to sleep above the shop. It had been a long night and they were all very tired. The following day the whole team gathered together for their first wireless contact with London, when they reported that fifty per cent of the parachutes attached to the packages of supplies had failed to open. Then they got down to the work of contacting the other circuits and the local maquis. Liewer had been expecting to find efficient groups of local resisters. The reality was somewhat different. In an undated report made by Liewer, probably at the end of August or beginning of September 1944, he explained what was happening in that part of France at that time;

> I would like to make clear the position and situation, which I found when I arrived in the BISTROT Maquis, and in the Haute Vienne, generally speaking, just after D-Day.
>
> When I left London I was given to understand that I would find on arrival a very well organised Maquis, strictly devoid of any political intrigues, which would constitute a very good basis for extending (the) circuit throughout the area.
>
> On arrival I did find a Maquis, which was roughly 600 strong, plus 200 gendarmes who joined up on D-Day; but these men were strictly not trained, and commanded by the most incapable people I have ever met; also most decided not to fight, as was overwhelmingly proved by the fact that: primo, none of the D-Day targets had been attended to; secundo: the following three weeks it each time took me several hours' discussions to get a small team out, either to the railway or to the telephone lines.

Liewer's report went on to explain that:

The chief of this Maquis, who calls himself Colonel CHARLES, was by trade a saxophonist in a Bal Musette, and a soldat 2ième classe, with no war experience. He had been for HECTOR, SAMUEL and ANASTASIE their only contact with the Maquis, which neither of them had ever really visited, relying on CHARLES for their information.

When I first met CHARLES he emphasised the fact that he and his Maquis were strictly unpolitical. I nevertheless discovered some time later that on the night of my arrival with my party, CHARLES had been round the billets which were assigned to us, revolver in hand, reminding everyone: 'Remember, we are not FTPs'.

The story in short is that CHARLES had been acting as decoy for George GUINGOIN, the local FTP leader.

When I finally met GUINGOIN after the first day operation on the 25th June, he was very bold and outspoken, in his desire to collaborate with me on the condition that I had no political motive; I was just as bold, and stated that I was only interested in winning the war, and that providing he undertook to attend to all targets which I might designate, I would arm his troops to the best of our ability.

After some arguing he accepted the agreement, and from that day he has <u>never</u> failed to execute immediately all orders from London, as well as to attend to all targets.

Liewer hoped that when he established contact with the other circuits in the area he would find that they had been better organized and run than the maquis.

(*Hector, Samuel* and *Anastasie* referred to above were the code names of Maurice Southgate, his assistant and a young Frenchman, Jacques Dufour, later to figure in Violette's story. The 'first day operation' to which Liewer referred was one of seventy-six supply drops organized by him in the months from June to September. This first drop, by the USAAF on 25 June, delivered 839 containers. Over the four-month period a total of 3695 containers and 562 packages were parachuted into the area to equip the circuits and the local maquis.)

After the garbled message given on p. 77 from Harry Peulevé's Author circuit had been received, stopping Violette and Liewer from going to Rouen, Peulevé was himself arrested on 21 March 1944. The Gestapo had received some information from one of his neighbours that there was a Jewish man using the house for black marketeering and were making a routine check when they came across Peulevé and his colleague, Roland Malraux, brother of Claude and André. They had been in wireless contact with London when the Gestapo agents broke into the house and Peulevé quickly tore off his silk code and tried to burn it, as he had been instructed. He was amazed to find that the silk wouldn't burn. With Peulevé in German hands, his assistant, Jacques Poirier, code name *Nestor*, had immediately taken over the circuit, which continued in the same manner as it had under its founder. However, with Poirier now in charge, the circuit name was changed to Digger.

In order to set up a meeting with Jacques Poirier, Liewer sent Violette to make the arrangements. It had been decided that she would set out early on the morning of 10 June. The previous evening she went for a walk in the company of Jean Claude Guiet. She wanted to know where he had set up his radio and he took her to where he was then staying. On the way they discussed many things. Violette was interested to know Guiet's first impressions of life as an agent and she told him of her admiration and respect for Liewer. She also told him that she believed that life was a chance and that one must take chances in life. She was determined that her life would make a difference. Then she told him that she had a lot of travelling to do the next day so had better get back to where she was staying and get everything ready for her journey. She said goodnight to Guiet. It was the last time he ever saw her.

The next morning she was up early. She had a journey of about 100 miles to cover and would be accompanied for the first part at least by Jacques Dufour, code name *Anastasie*, who had done a lot of work with the Stationer circuit and was now going to work with Liewer in Salesman. He had offered to drive her about half-way south with her bicycle strapped to the car, so that the journey wouldn't take her too long. She was, after all, quite used to cycling long distances, having done so many times in her teens as part of the cycle club.

Before they began their journey Violette spoke to Liewer about taking a weapon with her. She was most insistent that she should have a Sten gun and some ammunition and so he gave her the gun with two spare magazines.

At a distance of nearly sixty years, there is no way now of knowing for certain why Violette insisted on carrying the gun. There does, however, seem to be a link to what Bob Maloubier told me, that she was determined to kill some Germans because of the death of Etienne. She would almost certainly have been safer without the gun. Her cover story for her second mission was supposed to be that she was the widow of an *antiquaire* or antique dealer from Nantes and that her name was Mme Villeret. It is hard to imagine how she could have explained the fact that the widow of an antique dealer drove around the French countryside toting a semi-automatic weapon and still manage to convince the Germans that she posed them no threat. It would seem obvious that she had made up her mind that, given the opportunity, she would kill as many Germans as possible, regardless of the outcome and of her own personal safety. But she didn't seem to have a death wish at all. She was happy and cheerful. After the initial shock of Etienne's death, she had picked herself up and gradually got back into the swing of everyday life and, although she had her moments of depression, she was not a depressed person. Perhaps her hatred of the nation that had taken away her beloved husband was intensified because the Germans had also taken away the life that she and Etienne had planned for themselves and for Tania. With Etienne her life would have been very different. She would have been the wife of a career soldier living, perhaps, in exotic parts of the world, maybe even with servants to attend to the household chores that she so disliked. She would have had the support of her husband in bringing up their daughter and any other children they might have had later. Without Etienne she was just another widow with a baby, struggling to provide for what would probably be her only child and eking out an existence as a shop assistant, along with hundreds of other women in the same position as herself. Perhaps that was why, during her last few hours of freedom, she insisted on carrying a gun.

Having strapped her bicycle to the car and put her Sten gun and spare magazines in a safe place in the car, Violette and Dufour began their journey. Their planned route was to take them first to La Croisille sur Briance where Dufour wanted to pick up a fellow maquisard, Jean Bariaud, who would keep him company on the return trip. R.J. Minney in *Carve Her Name with Pride* described Bariaud as the son of the local doctor, a boy of not quite twelve years old. He was, in fact, twenty-six years old on that June day of 1944 and the bicycle that was roped to the car in Minney's description belonged to Violette and not to Bariaud.

Having fetched Bariaud the three proceeded along the road towards the village of Salon-la-Tour. As they approached the village they could see, ahead of them at the crossroads, that the Germans had mounted a roadblock. They were in a very difficult situation. The village was a quiet little place. If they were to turn around the Germans would undoubtedly see them; they were in a petrol-driven car, a large black Citröen, probably the same car that had fetched Violette and the other members of the Salesman team from the dropping zone outside Sussac three days before. Since many of the locals could only manage to run their cars with gas- or wood-burning boilers, the car itself was noteworthy, and in addition Violette was carrying a Sten gun and Dufour was also armed. The least suspicious member of the party was Bariaud, who, seeing the danger ahead, made up his mind to escape as soon as Dufour brought the car to a standstill.

The following report was made by Philippe Liewer, in which he says:

> Following is the report which DUFOUR gave me, to the best of my recollection.
>
> DUFOUR: We stopped at the first village on our way, namely La Croisille, to collect my friend Barriaud, who could thus keep me company on the way back; later, Barriaud climbed in the rear seat and I drove on, Szabo sitting beside me in front.
>
> Nearing the village of Salon, we came, after a bend in the road, to a T junction. At a distance of fifty yards, I saw we were coming to a road block, manned by German soldiers who waved me to stop. I instantly put out my arm and waved

back, slowed down, and warned Szabo to get prepared to jump out and run.

I stopped at thirty yards distance from the road block, jumped flat on the road surface by the car, and started shooting – I noticed Barriaud, who was unarmed, running away, but found that Szabo had taken up a similar position to mine on the other side of the car, and was firing too.

By that time though, one of the three Germans had been hit; the other two were spraying us generously. I ordered Szabo to retreat through a wheat field, towards a wood four hundred yards away, under cover of my fire. As soon as she had reached the high wheat she resumed firing, and I took advantage of it to fall back.

At first the going was good, as we walked, bending so as not to show our heads over the top of the wheat, but soon we heard the rumble of armoured cars, and machine guns began spraying close to us, as they could follow our progress by the movement of the wheat. So we had to continue our progress towards the wood crawling flat and cautiously on the ground, an exhausting and awfully slow process.

Then we heard infantry running up the road and entering the wheat field while other armoured cars went driving around it. So we had to resume firing each in turn to cover the other's progress, to keep the infantrymen from running up to us.

When we weren't more than thirty yards from the edge of the wood Szabo, who by then had her clothes all ripped to ribbons and was bleeding from numerous scratches all over her legs, told me she was exhausted and could not go an inch further.

She insisted she wanted me to try and get away, that there was no point in my staying with her. So I went on while she kept on firing from time to time and I managed to hide under a haystack in the courtyard of a small farm.

Last I know was that half an hour later Szabo was brought to that very farm by Germans; I heard them questioning her as to my whereabouts, and heard her answering, laughing 'You can run after him, he is far away by now'.

There is no mention in the account of Violette having sprained her ankle during the attempted escape. However, eyewitnesses have spoken of her limping while being taken away by German soldiers. This limp is probably best explained in an account given by Mme Montintin, whose daughter, Suzanne, had helped to hide Dufour under what she described as a pile of logs and he called a haystack. (Both accounts were translated from the French and possibly lost something in the translation.) Mme Montintin said:

> As soon as the Germans saw the car, they started to machine gun. They (*Violette Szabo and Jacques Dufour*) defended themselves like lions. Jacques shot until his last bullet and they had nothing left. The Germans injured the lady on the ankle with a bullet. She couldn't walk – that's when they caught her.
>
> A German officer approached and offered her a cigarette. She spat in his face and didn't accept it. She was very brave to do that. They took her to Germany – that is where she suffered and died.

There have been those who have accused both Dufour and Bariaud of cowardice in leaving a woman to fend for herself in the face of German aggression. Bariaud certainly seemed to have no other choice, as he was unarmed and therefore unable to assist his companions. Had he remained with them he would probably have done more harm than good and would have stretched their resources even further in an attempt to cover three and not two people.

As for Dufour, at that stage he probably had little choice either and it does seem as if Violette didn't want him to stay with her and risk being caught. He was very young, only twenty or twenty-one years old, and was said by the local people who knew him to have been hot-headed. He was known by many of the locals as he had lived in Salon-la-Tour for at least two years. The general feeling was that he had not properly planned the car journey. He had not taken any precautions against the possibility of running into German troops and yet he must have known that they were swarming all over the countryside on their way to Normandy to deal with the Allied landings there. He was, however, a very experienced member of the Resistance, having also worked closely with Maurice Southgate in his Stationer circuit liaising between members of the circuit and the local maquis. When Southgate was arrested he continued to liaise with other groups in the area and to do so until D-Day when he began his work in the Haute Vienne, joining the Salesman circuit when the team arrived on 8 June.

There was, however, serious friction between Dufour and Philippe Liewer, which may or may not have contributed to his actions on 10 June. In a report sent by Dufour to Colonel Maurice Buckmaster on 4 October 1944, he explained that:

> Up until that day I always worked in perfect harmony and with the perfect trust of all the agents in the service. But from the minute *Hamlet* arrived that trust and harmony disappeared.
>
> I introduced *Hamlet* to Charles Goumondie and all the maquis leaders. I warned him about the matter of communist politics in Limousin. He replied, 'On the matter of the FTP I am very clear.' From that day he excluded me from all discussions about the Resistance, from the point of view of organization, arms and politics.
>
> *Hamlet* is the sort of go-getter who would crush all those around him in order to elevate himself. After the first meeting that he had with Colonel Guingoin, FTP communist and head of one of the most important maquis, he, himself, said to me, 'Guingoin didn't hide from me that as well as the war against the Germans, he was also fighting another war elsewhere; the FTP have a great thing – an ideal'.
>
> That didn't stop *Hamlet* from supplying arms en masse to his groups who, at the same time, were using these arms for their own revolution, a familiar method employed by the leaders of the FTP.
>
> I condemn this action of *Hamlet's* because he did it completely out of the blue and I'll go further and say perhaps out of his own self-interest.
>
> The behaviour of *Hamlet* towards me: he took me for a complete idiot and passed me off as one in the eyes of everyone else and he treated me as one would treat an idiot.

The man who drove Violette into the roadblock that day was obviously not happy and it is easy to imagine the frustration he must have felt when he realized that his actions had probably proved that Liewer was right in thinking him an idiot. Whether or not Liewer really did think of him as such is another matter. I did not find a single criticism of Dufour in any of the reports by Liewer that I came across. That, of course, does not mean that there weren't any, but perhaps it was merely the younger man's pride, dented by not being included in the discussions about Resistance policy, that made him feel this way.

It must have been a relief to Violette to be able to look at a German and not have to hide her genuine reaction to him, as she had had to do in Rouen during her first mission. Now that she had been caught she was happy for the Germans to know how much she despised them. Another eyewitness has said that she shouted at her captors to get away from her and leave her arms free so that she could get one of her own cigarettes. The German in charge of the roadblock is said to have told her that she was the bravest woman he had ever seen. He then saluted her, not a Nazi salute but a smart military salute, before ordering her to be taken away. Following the arrest she was taken to Gestapo headquarters in Limoges, from where she was transferred to Limoges prison in the Place du Champ de Foire on the following day, 11 June. She gave her name as Vicky Taylor, which was the name she had intended to use if it had been necessary at any time for her to escape overland and get back to England via Spain. Why she picked that name is unknown, although it could have been a play on her own name, as *szabo* is the Hungarian word for tailor.

When Jean Bariaud managed to get to Sussac he immediately raised the alarm about Violette and Dufour. Liewer contacted Jean Claude Guiet to ask when his next schedule was and the shocked Guiet coded the first of many messages that he was to send to London regarding Violette's capture. Sadly none of these messages seems to have survived. Jean Claude Guiet told me:

> It was not until October, in Paris, as I was returning to England that I found out that Corinne was Violette Szabo,

> and not until several years later that I found out about her fate and her previous operations.

The team did consider a rescue attempt but there was no time to plan one as on 12 June, the day after Violette had been taken to Limoges prison, she was again taken away and, this time, no one in her team knew where she had gone.

Chapter Nine

Captivity

The soldiers who had mounted the roadblock and who captured Violette were members of the 2nd SS Panzer Division *Das Reich*. They had been on their way to Normandy from their headquarters in Montauban, in the département of Tarn et Garonne north of Toulouse, when a number of them were ordered to the village of Guéret where the German garrison had been surrounded by maquisards. *SS Sturmbannführer* Helmut Kämpfe of the 3rd Armoured Battalion commanded this group. During the course of the fighting that ensued, thirty-one maquisards were killed. While returning to join the rest of the division on the night of 9–10 June, *Sturmbannführer* Kämpfe was kidnapped by maquisards at a tiny village called La Bussière, south-east of Limoges. His captor was Sergeant Jean Canou of the FTP.

When it became clear to the Germans that something had happened to Kämpfe they began to search for him. The roadblock in Salon-la-Tour was just one of many that they manned the day after Kämpfe disappeared, in an attempt to find him. By then, however, he had been passed on to Georges Guingoin, leader of the FTP group. He, hearing about the deaths of the thirty-one maquisards, decided to execute Kämpfe. Had the kidnap not taken place Violette would not have been stopped at the roadblock and perhaps this story would have had a different ending.

SS Sturmbannführer Adolf Diekmann was a personal friend of Helmut Kämpfe. He was furious when he heard what had happened to his friend and organized a terrible reprisal. He went to the village of Oradour-sur-Glane to the north-west of Limoges.

Separating the men of the village from the women and children, he locked the latter in the church. He then had the men shot and the church set on fire: 646 people died and the village was ransacked. To this day Oradour-sur-Glane remains as it was left on that terrible day in June 1944, a memorial to the people and a reminder of the barbarity of which the human race is capable.

The one consolation was that the incident delayed the *Das Reich* division for forty-eight hours while they searched for Kämpfe. The journey from Montauban to the Normandy coast, which should have taken about seventy-two hours, was extended finally to over two weeks, as a result of this incident and many other diversions planned by various Resistance groups.

The Salesman team, although distressed by the capture of their courier, still had work to do. In March 1944 de Gaulle, in London, had set up the FFI, the *Forces Françaises de l'Intérieur*, which he intended as the army of the new France and which would unite all resisters in France, whatever their political persuasion, in the common goal of freeing the country from enemy occupation. The overall commander of this force was de Gaulle's friend and supporter, General Marie-Pierre Koenig, formerly of the 13 DBLE. Part of Liewer's mission was to ensure that all resisting forces in the Salesman area adhered to de Gaulle's directive. In a report sent to London, he explained the difficulties he had had to this end:

> From the end of June I lived in daily contact with GUINGOIN, and constantly kept his mind at the goal of unification under the FFI banner. The département of Haute Vienne possesses the peculiarity of holding a large majority of FTP Maquis; therefore the point of view of the FTP leaders was that, whereas in other departments such as Creuse, for instance, where the FTPs are a minority and the FFI chief belongs to the A.S. *(Armée Secrète)* organisation, and where the FTPs have accepted to work under his command, in Haute Vienne the command should be given to them. Late in July this point of view was adopted as well by Colonel RIVIER, Chef d'Etat Major, Region Cinq.

Amazingly, even though the various Resistance groups were all working for a common goal, their progress was often slowed down by in-fighting caused by idealistic differences. On 16 September 1944 this same Colonel Rivier was to sign the citation awarding the *Croix de Guerre* with Silver Star to Enseigne Vicky Taylor, alias Violette Szabo. (see Appendix B)

Throughout June Liewer and Maloubier organized the training of many of the members of the Bistrot maquis in the Haute Vienne, which after D-Day numbered about 800, having been joined by approximately 200 gendarmes on 6 June. They armed selected groups of saboteurs who cut the electricity supplies for the submarine base at Rochefort and blew up the railway lines connecting Paris and Limoges and the lines between Bordeaux and Toulouse. When the Germans began to repair the track Liewer arranged for the derailment of two trains in a deep cutting at Salon-la-Tour, which blocked the line for two months. Maloubier blew up bridges, placing a charge at each end and one in the middle; placed thus the structure spiralled up into the air. Maloubier says that on his best day he blew up and destroyed seven bridges!

In July men of the Salesman circuit and the associated maquis were involved in fighting near Châteauneuf, with 3000 troops composed of SS, Infantry and French militiamen. Two hundred and fifty enemy troops were killed, including twelve officers, for the loss of only thirty-two Frenchmen.

During August more sabotage of the railway system was carried out with an armoured train being attacked by Liewer and his men in association with members of the SAS. At the same time maquisards from the 'Garage' maquis group in Corrèze dumped hundreds of tons of rocks onto the line between Uzerche and Brive, stopping another armoured train from getting through.

On 21 August Liewer led an Allied delegation of four officers who forced the German Commander of Limoges, General Gleiniger, to surrender unconditionally, along with his garrison of 1500 men. Liewer and his colleagues had finally liberated the town.

Philippe Liewer was awarded the *Croix de Guerre* on 16 September, the same day that Violette was awarded her *Croix de Guerre*, and in October he returned to England to be awarded the Military Cross.

He sent his last message to London, dated 2 September 1944, concerning the fate of his courier, Violette Szabo, whom he still called Louise. In it he said:

> About Louise, all I have been able to ascertain is that she was taken to Limoges on the 11th of June and out of it on the 12th. Her destination is unknown, but I am afraid she is more likely to have been shot than taken to Germany. She gave as an identity her name for Spain.

Having returned to England, Liewer made a report, dated 12 October 1944, in which he recommended awards to be made to certain members of both his Salesman circuit and to French members of maquis groups in Haute Vienne and Corrèze. With the exception of his citation for Violette, which is given here, the text of all the other citations can be found in Appendix C, at the end of the book.

Liewer begins his report, entitled CITATIONS FOR DECORATIONS, by recommending:

> Highest possible decorations for holders of British commissions for:-
>
> Mrs ZABO, (sic) my courier. On 10th June 1944, at 11a.m. she came against a German road block near SALON-LA-TOUR (Corrèze). She was riding in a car driven by ANASTASIE. With great coolness and gallantry she fought it out for 20 minutes with her Sten gun, covering ANASTASIE while he was retreating, and being covered by him while she was retreating through fields. She only surrendered being completely exhausted and short of ammunition, and she is believed to have killed one German.

Contrary to Liewer's belief that Violette had been shot, she had, in fact, been taken from Limoges prison to Fresnes on the outskirts of Paris.

In Limoges *SS Sturmbannführer* Kowatch, who usually conducted the interrogation of prisoners, probably interrogated her. As Liewer said in his report she gave her name as Vicky

Taylor, the name she planned to use if she had to escape via Spain. It is likely that this is why her *Croix de Guerre* was awarded in the name of Taylor, with her real name being shown as an alias.

She was quickly transferred to Fresnes, and from there was taken to SD headquarters at 84 avenue Foch, the wide, elegant, tree-lined avenue leading from the Place de l'Etoile towards the Bois de Boulogne. Here *SS Sturmbannführer* Kieffer would have interrogated her. In spite of claims to the contrary, notably by R.J. Minney in *Carve Her Name With Pride*, but also by others, I have not been able to find any conclusive proof that she was ever tortured. Certainly if she were going to be tortured it would have been in the avenue Foch, where many prisoners received the special SD treatment, and it would have been at the start of her imprisonment when any information she might be able to give would still have a value. But there is no record of any ill treatment and there are witness statements from those who shared her cell in Fresnes. It would have been hard to hide something like that from her fellow prisoners and, indeed, why would she want to? M.R.D. Foot in his book *SOE in France*, part of the official History of the Second World War published by HMSO, has said that he found no evidence of any torture of the women agents. After his book was published Odette Churchill (later Hallowes) GC, code name *Lise*, who insisted that she had been tortured, challenged him in court and he was forced to edit the second edition of the book to reflect this. Of Violette, Foot says:

> One tale of torture deserves particular notice, for it is only a tale. The ghastly story of Violette Szabo's sufferings, published in her mother's and her daughter's lifetime, is so far as I can ascertain completely fictitious: no other evidence I have seen suggests that she was ever subjected to personal violence at all.

It is comforting to know that others believe, as I do, that Violette was not tortured. Unlike Professor Foot, I do believe that she may have been subjected to some personal violence, but nothing that could be described as torture. I certainly don't think that the lack of torture detracts in any way from the courage shown by Violette

Szabo during her time in captivity. Even if she were not tortured she would still have had to live with the fear that she might be and the treatment that she did suffer was extremely unpleasant. As will be shown, she bore her suffering with great fortitude.

There were a number of cells at the premises in avenue Foch where prisoners were kept for interrogation and, after the war, Violette's name and the date 5 June 1944 were found on the wall of cell number 45. Since she was still in England on 5 June it is likely that the date should have been 15 June and that the number 1 had been erased somehow. She was not held at avenue Foch for any length of time, but would probably have been taken there at least two or three times at the start of her imprisonment at Fresnes.

Fresnes was a huge prison that had been built to replace three other prisons in Paris. Mazas on boulevard Diderot, Ste. Pélagie on rue de la Chef and la Roquette, close to the Bastille were all closed down once Fresnes came into being and it took in its first prisoners in 1898. It was an imposing, sinister-looking place. Beneath the rows of cells were dank, dark dungeons that during the German occupation were often used to punish a prisoner for some supposed misdeed. Anyone subjected to this treatment was kept entirely in the dark, was unlikely to be given a bed or proper toilet facilities and had to live in a cell where the walls were covered with slime and mildew.

During August and September 1947 the RAF representative in France and a Frenchwoman, Mme G. Meunier, exchanged some correspondence regarding the graves of three RAF men who had been shot down at Quiberon. In the course of a letter written by Mme Meunier on 11 September she suddenly mentioned that:

> I have read in the French papers, few days ago, some information about the 'French section' which have reminded me of certain details, and I think useful to tell you about it.
>
> When I was in jail during the German Occupation, in the 'Fresnes' prison, cell No. 435, one of my companions was a young lady, Violette Szabo, English parachutist of the French Section, and I am relating on a separate sheet the facts and circumstances concerning her arrest, as she herself explained to me about it.

Mme Meunier began her account with some general details. She said that Violette told her she was twenty-three years old, that she had been called 'Louise', that she had a French mother and an English father, that she had been married and widowed, that her husband was of Hungarian origin and she had a daughter of about two or three years old back in England. She also mentioned a brother or sister, Mme Meunier couldn't remember which, back in England. She described Violette as being, 'About 1m 75. Very slim – Very dark hair and eyes – Gipsy type, very good looking.'

These details would seem to prove that Mme Meunier had, indeed, met and conversed with Violette. They are mostly accurate with the exception of Violette's age and perhaps her height. She was actually only twenty-two at this point and a few centimetres shorter than Mme Meunier claimed. Although she had four brothers and not one, the three older boys were all away in the armed services by 1944 and so she did only have one brother at home in England at that point, nine-year-old Richard.

Having established the basic details, Mme Meunier continued her story, which was, at times, muddled and inaccurate. However, as she said in her letter, 'I am at your entire disposal for all information you could ask for, though my memory is very bad, I think I have forgotten nothing of what I know.' It must be remembered that Mme Meunier was telling the story in late 1947 of someone she had met in mid-1944. In addition she was in a ghastly place during the time her account took place and went on to suffer even more when she was sent to Ravensbrück concentration camp. Small wonder there were inaccuracies in her account. I have been able to highlight some of the discrepancies in her story. Readers must decide for themselves whether or not what remains is accurate.

Violette, she said, belonged to the 'French Section' and had been parachuted three times into France, the last time being in May 1944. She said that at that time, Violette had all her luggage with her, as she did not intend to go back to England. She was carrying a large amount of money, as was her 'Chief' who parachuted into France with her, along with another young man of about twenty who was, she believed, of Northern origin and was called Christian. About three days after they arrived the Germans surrounded the maquis and, although they fought with their guns, they eventually had to give themselves up. Violette, her 'Chief' and the young man were taken to several jails before being taken to Limoges.

Violette was, of course, parachuted into France on two occasions, not three, the last time being in June and not May 1944. It is likely that she did have a significant amount of money with her, as her 'Chief' would have had. He did parachute in with her, as did a young man of about twenty. Bob Maloubier was twenty; Jean Claude Guiet was nineteen. Three days after their arrival Violette herself was arrested but not the others. There were, however, three people in the car when they reached the roadblock at Salon-la-Tour and there was a gunfight. Violette herself was taken to Gestapo headquarters and to Limoges prison, which could possibly account for the story of 'several jails'.

Mme Meunier's account continues:

> The fact which impressed Violette the most was that, as soon as in possession of their identity, the Germans told them that the said identity was false, indicating to each of them their real name. This fact made Violette think that the real information concerning the parachutage had been given to the Germans, with perfect and precise knowledge of the names, date of birth, date of the parachutage, and of the duty to be fulfilled. Young Violette, all these evidences being given to her had to admit that she was in fact Violette SZABO, and not Louise X . . . *(This, of course, was not accurate, as Violette had given her name as Vicky Taylor, not as Louise.)*
>
> Having been brought to Paris, avenue Foch, she was given a suit-case containing some effects, as her personal belongings had been stolen while she was in the country. However, when she arrived in the FRESNES jail, she was wearing the same dress as when she left London: a new one, in crepe de chine, with blue and white flowers. Her shoes were of blue leather, wedge heel type, made in Paris during a former stay. She was also wearing a shirt in black crepe georgette, with yellow lace, this being one of her personal belongings.
>
> She was incarcerated in my cell No. 435, 4th floor, 3rd Division, German Section. Until I left, when I was deported to Germany, she was never questioned any more (until 7 July

> 1944). She used to repeat: 'I know who has denounced us. He is a member of the French section, he is, at the moment in London, and he is the one who told the Germans about our real identity.'
>
> Her greatest sorrow was to think that this traitor was given full confidence and was so able to carry on his treachery.
>
> According to information given by some companions of Deportation, she is said to have been sent to RAVENSBRÜCK the 10th August 1944, and killed there few months later (spring of 1945).
>
> Personally, I cannot say anything about her deportation, as I left RAVENSBRÜCK the 7th Aug. 1944, being sent to the Salt Mines of BEENDORF.

It was a standard German trick to try to convince captured agents that there was a traitor in their midst, recruited by the German authorities but living and working in London at the heart of SOE. After his arrest, Harry Peulevé was interrogated in Tulle prior to being taken to Limoges and on to Paris. His report describes what happened there:

> During this interrogation I was shown pictures of amongst others Prosper (*Francis Suttill*) and details of his circuit. Amongst other photographs and maps they showed me were particulars about S.T.S. training schools in England. This was obviously to convince me that they knew everything about our organisation and of course I realised that it was quite easy for them to obtain this information and it did not convince me in the slightest.

As Duncan Stuart, SOE Advisor at the Foreign & Commonwealth Office, told me, 'If Mme Meunier's account of what SZABO told her is accurate and if, therefore, the Germans in Limoges really did know SZABO's real name, then they clearly had a good penetration source, but all other evidence suggests that this would have been in France.'

Very few people would have known Violette's true identity. The details on the citation for her Croix de Guerre give her name as Vicky Taylor, alias Violette Szabo, and Liewer knew that she used this name when arrested, as was shown in his message to London dated 2 September 1944. He would also have known that her real name was Violette Szabo. Bob Maloubier knew her real name. He had been introduced to her family and the letter she wrote to him on 11 March 1944 was signed 'Violette'. Jean Claude Guiet, Salesman's wireless operator, did not find out Violette's true identity until he was in Paris in October 1944, on his way back to England. Jacques Dufour knew her as Louise, but in the report he gave to Philippe Liewer about the ambush in Salon-la-Tour, he refers to her as Szabo. There is, of course, absolutely no suggestion that either Liewer or Maloubier gave her name to the German authorities. However, the names on the citation for her Croix de Guerre would seem to suggest that Mme Meunier's story about the Germans in Limoges having her correct name is true. Just as the Germans had informers, so too did the French and it would seem likely that when it was decided to award Violette the Croix de Guerre her name was obtained, through an informer, from the German authorities who had arrested her. Had either Liewer or Maloubier given the name for her citation, they would surely have just called her Violette Szabo. The name of Vicky Taylor, although known by Liewer, was not relevant and there would have been no advantage in perpetuating the myth of her being Vicky Taylor and then giving her correct name alongside it.

This, of course, leaves the problem of whether or not the traitor was in France, as has been suggested as being more likely by Duncan Stuart, or if, as Violette believed, it was someone in London. Since there is no written record of a name in Mme Meunier's account it is difficult to know who Violette thought it might be. There were people in SOE who, either by design or by accident, did give away the names of other agents or other secret information. The names of John Starr, Henri Déricourt and Nicholas Bodington, who was a friend of both Déricourt and *SS Sturmbannführer* Karl Boemelburg, spring to mind. Boemelburg was Commandant at Gestapo headquarters at 82 avenue Foch, next door to SD headquarters where Violette was interrogated. It is difficult, however, to see how any of these three could have been involved and there may, of course, have been others.

It is likely that Violette's imagination was working overtime in trying to discover who had betrayed her. With so much time on her hands and nothing else to do, she probably came to a number of different conclusions and it is unlikely that we will ever discover who it was that she believed to be the culprit.

Mme Meunier's letter giving all her recollections of the conversations she had with Violette was received by the RAF representative in France and passed on to the War Office, SOE having been disbanded by this time. The SOE Liquidation Officer, Major Norman Mott, wrote a reply to Mme Meunier dated 14 October 1947 in which he said:

> Your letter dated 11th September, 1947, in which you give certain information regarding Violette Szabo, has been passed to this Department of the War Office by the Air Ministry as Mme. Szabo was in the employ of this Department as a member of the 'French Section' of the War Office at the time she was arrested in France in 1944.
>
> Although the information which you have so kindly given does not include any facts previously unknown to us, we are, nevertheless, most grateful to you for the kindly thought which prompted you to bring it to the notice of the representative of the Royal Air Force in France.
>
> It is, unfortunately, quite true that Mme. Szabo was eventually executed at Ravensbruck in the Spring of 1945; and you may be interested to learn that in recognition of the gallant way in which she fulfilled her mission in France she has been posthumously awarded the George Cross which, as you probably know, is one of our highest British decorations.

This reply would seem to be just a polite acknowledgment of Mme Meunier's letter rather than an admission that certain of the 'facts' were true. There appears to have been no other follow-up and the matter was regarded as having been dealt with.

The Germans were in the habit not only of planting ideas of treachery in the heads of their prisoners but also of moving their prisoners around a lot, probably to deny them any kind of comfort that might be gained from establishing friendships but also to try to glean any information that might be available when the prisoners went through introductions and swapping of stories with new cell mates.

At some point during the middle of July 1944 Violette was moved from the cell she had shared with Mme Meunier until her departure for Ravensbrück on 7 July, to another cell, number 24, which was located on the third floor of the prison building. She shared this cell with an elderly portrait artist, and another Frenchwoman, Marie Lecomte, soon joined them there. The latter arrived at eleven o'clock one night, having been brought from the prison in Brest where she had been condemned to death for her Resistance activities near to her home in Morlaix in Brittany. Marie was forty years old when she met Violette and the two women came to regard each other as surrogate mother and daughter. Violette called Mme Lecomte 'Maman Marie' and referred to her as her second mother. There was an iron staircase close to their cell and when they heard the guards' heavy footsteps on the iron steps they would hold their breath and pray that the steps would not stop at their door. Of course it was inevitable that one day a guard did come and Violette was taken away.

Marie had been beaten when she was arrested by the Gestapo and arrived at Fresnes with her face covered in cuts and bruises. In a letter written to Violette's parents after the war she told them that she believed Violette had been at Fresnes about ten days when she herself arrived. That would make her arrival date somewhere around 23 June, at a time when Violette was sharing her cell with Mme Meunier. It is possible that both Violette and Mme Meunier had been moved to the cell on the lower floor and that Mme Meunier was the elderly portrait artist. Unfortunately Marie Lecomte is no longer alive and I have been unable to discover anything about Mme Meunier other than the details given to me by the SOE advisor. If Mme Meunier was the artist, she made no mention of it in her letter in 1947, nor did she say anything about having shared the cell with anyone other than Violette, although this may have been because her letter was written to the British authorities and Marie Lecomte was French. She, likewise, did not mention in her letter anything about Mme Meunier. It is obviously also possible that Marie Lecomte was mistaken about the date of her arrival and that she actually got to Fresnes after Mme Meunier had left.

Although some of the details that she recounted are muddled, it would seem that the basic story she gave as having been told to her by Violette is true. She did say that when Violette was caught at the roadblock her male companion was also caught and they were both brutally assaulted. Since Dufour was not caught, there is doubt that any of that part of her story is correct, although when she spoke of the assault she may have been referring to Violette having been shot in the ankle as described by Mme Montintin.

Some of the male prisoners in Fresnes were allowed an exercise period in the yard below the window of Violette's cell. Marie Lecomte tells how she and Violette watched them:

> With a piece of whale bone from my corsets we made a small pin sharp enough to pierce the glass; we could see with one eye to it what was going on. One day Violette saw a man who had worked with her. She said, 'I must send a message somehow.' I got up on the head of the iron bed, took the stiff curtain to make a funnel of it and shouted through it – 'all is well V – all is well V'. Violette looking at the hole saw him look up, he had heard. We did not see him again.

Perhaps something has been lost in the translation here as it is difficult to imagine the Germans hanging curtains at the cell windows. The man to whom Marie Lecomte referred may have been Harry Peulevé as he was part of a large group which was taken from Fresnes at the same time that Violette left the prison herself and they had known each other slightly before coming to France.

With Violette during July 1944 was Mme Wimille, wife of Jean-Paul Wimille of the old Chestnut circuit, which had been led by the English racing driver, Charles Grover-Williams, code name *Sebastien*. M.R.D. Foot described in *SOE in France* how when Mme Wimille was taken to the Gare de l'Est to be deported to Germany she saw her cousin driving a Red Cross van and, when no one was looking, jumped into the van, put on a white coat and began serving sandwiches until it was safe for her to leave. This may even have been at the same time that Violette began her long journey to Germany.

Marie Lecomte said in her letter to Violette's parents that Violette left Fresnes on 13 August and that she, herself, left two days later on the 15th. She remembered the dates because her birthday was 15 August. There was, however, another report, which was found on Violette's personal file. It was written by Mlle Rosier and dated August 1945 (thirteen years before Marie Lecomte's letter was written) which said:

> . . . on 8 August 1944, seven girls left Fresnes chained together. They passed through Neurenn, near Saarbrücken, and arrived at Ravensbrück on 25 August 1944. One of the 3 English girls was described as Corinne or Violette, small, dark, large eyes, said to have been arrested in a maquis at Limoges.

If, as seems likely, it was Violette who left in this group, then the other two 'English' girls must have been Denise Bloch and Lilian Rolfe, who ultimately suffered the same fate as she did. Denise was, of course, French and not English but she was employed by SOE and held a commission in the FANYs, so was probably thought of as 'English'. Another SOE agent thought to have been in the same party was a WAAF officer, the half-Indian, half-American Noor Inayat Khan, code name *Madeleine*, whose final destination was Dachau near Munich, where, on 12 or 13 September, she was executed by a shot in the back of the neck.

When she left Fresnes, Violette was put into chains that consisted of a heavy bangle around her wrist and a similar one around her ankle. The two bangles were joined by a very short chain, which meant that she was unable to walk in an upright position. She was also chained to another prisoner, making movements very difficult. The men who were being deported at this time were also chained, two by two.

All the prisoners were assembled in the main hall at Fresnes, prior to being taken to the Gare de l'Est from where they were put on a train to Saarbrücken in Germany. While they were standing around, many of them recognized each other. For some it was the first sight of a familiar face that they had had in many months. At the station they were put into separate compartments. The men were locked in a prison carriage while the women sat in ordinary third class compartments. *Feldgendarmerie* guarded them, with a Gestapo officer from the office at avenue Foch in charge of the convoy.

The train travelled very slowly through the French countryside for the remainder of the day and night and into the next afternoon. Then at about 2 p.m. when they had reached Châlons-sur-Marne the train came under attack by Allied bombers. The male prisoners were locked into their compartment and there was a fear of being burned alive if the carriage was hit. The German guards had left the train but had threatened to shoot anyone who tried to escape. While the train was being bombed Violette and her chained companion fetched water supplies for the men who had not had anything to drink for many hours.

In his book *The White Rabbit* Bruce Marshall tells the story of the legendary Forest Frederick Edward Yeo-Thomas of RF Section, who was also on the train that day. He says that Yeo-Thomas prayed that the carriage would not be hit by an incendiary and continues:

> His fear seemed to communicate itself to his companions for he felt a painful wrench at his wrist as he was jerked forward by his twin on top of a mass of bodies seeking cover from the shells and the machine-gun bullets. They were all rather ashamed of their panic when, a few minutes later, Violet (sic) Szabo and another girl came crawling along the corridor to bring them water.

Coincidentally, before the war Edward Molyneux had employed Yeo-Thomas at his salon at 5 rue Royale where, a few months before their only meeting, Violette had bought the three dresses and the golf jersey.

R.J. Minney has described the same incident somewhat differently. His rather xenophobic account has a number of Belgians and Frenchmen becoming hysterical, flinging themselves on top of each other and frothing at the mouth. He also describes in detail the reaction of Harry Peulevé both when he saw Violette on the train and later when the entire group had to spend the night in stables attached to the barracks he claims were in Metz. Violette and Harry are supposed to have talked through the night about old times and their experiences in France. Peulevé is quoted as saying:

> But either through modesty or a sense of delicacy, since some of the tortures were too intimate in their application or perhaps because she did not wish to live again through the pain of it, she spoke hardly at all about the tortures she had been made to suffer. She was in a cheerful mood. Her spirits were high. She was confident of victory and was resolved on escaping no matter where they took her.

Minney then says:

> Thus, in the darkness, with each chained by the ankle to another and the drain between them, they had their last romantic interchanges, with their hopes and dreams unvoiced but no doubt shared.

Harry Peulevé is mentioned in the acknowledgments in *Carve Her Name With Pride*, so it would seem that he spoke to Minney about what happened that day. His own account, however, written on 23 April 1945 and found in the Public Record Office, merely says:

> I left Fresnes on the 10th August and was taken from solitary confinement to a cell where I met other agents. In all we left Paris 37 strong, mostly from Fresnes but with a few who came from avenue Foch or Compiègne. . . .
>
> We travelled all night until two o'clock next afternoon when the train was bombed by Allied planes and brought to a standstill. Luckily we had no casualties either amongst the women or ourselves, but seventeen German soldiers being evacuated to Germany were killed and one British prisoner of war. I believe we were in the vicinity of Châlons-sur-Marne and from there we continued our journey in a requisitioned lorry to Reims, having been told that should one escape everybody would be shot. I nevertheless made every attempt to free myself from the handcuffs and had agreed with the other man to whom I was handcuffed, whose

> name was Barrett, that we should attempt to escape. Unfortunately, the majority of prisoners saw that we were attempting to escape and said that we should not as we should be endangering everybody's lives. We stayed the night in large barracks in Reims and the next morning continued our journey in the lorry and here I managed to get my handcuffs off.

Although one would not expect Peulevé to wax lyrical about Violette in an official report, one would have thought that, had they been having the sort of relationship hinted at by Minney and in view of her bravery on the train, he might well have given her a passing mention. In spite of an extensive search, I have not been able to uncover one shred of evidence of a romantic liaison between Violette and Peulevé. If one existed it has remained very well hidden. Jean Overton Fuller has said in her fascinating book *The German Penetration of SOE* that Peulevé was in love with Violette. However, she did not say that there was a romance between them and as someone who has studied the people and goings-on of SOE said to me when I inquired if he knew of a romance, 'Half the men who met Violette Szabo were probably "in love" with her; she was after all an exceptionally attractive girl.'

Having spent the night in stables, the prisoners, both men and women, were herded onto trucks the next morning to be taken to Metz and then to Saarbrücken. When they arrived the men and women were separated and did not come into contact with each other again.

The camp at Saarbrücken was called Neue Bremm. It was a small and particularly cruel place. Between October 1941 and November 1944 it handled 146 convoys of female prisoners from France bound for Ravensbrück, eighty going through during 1944 alone. A total of 10,000 French prisoners passed through the camp on their way to Ravensbrück, including common criminals, resistance fighters and Jews. The length of their stay at Neue Bremm depended on the number of prisoners arriving with each transport. They remained there until there were enough of them to fill the cattle trucks that were used for their onward journey.

Although most prisoners went through the camp quite quickly some unfortunate women had to remain there for as long as a month. Because it was a place where no one stayed for long there were no facilities at all and the food was nothing more than a few dried crusts of bread, which were thrown at the women, who had to fight to get them. It is doubtful whether it was ever worth the fight as the scraps were usually inedible. Women who stayed there for any length of time emerged weak and emaciated. Neue Bremm was undoubtedly the place that Mlle Rosier meant when she referred to Neurenn in her report of August 1945.

Violette must have remained in Saarbrücken in these terrible conditions for approximately ten days before beginning the journey eastwards towards Berlin, packed into a cattle truck with hardly room to move, much less sit or lie down. She and Yvonne Baseden met up briefly in Saarbrücken. They had last met when Violette had taken Tania to one of the SOE offices. After two or three days Violette left for Ravensbrück and by the time Yvonne arrived there she had already been moved on. They did not see each other again. Yvonne survived the horrors of Ravensbrück and just before the end of the war, when she was very ill, the Swedish Red Cross rescued her and a number of other prisoners and eventually arranged her return journey to England.

Violette now spent her time with two new companions, Denise Bloch and Lilian Rolfe. In contrast to the more famous women who worked with SOE, very little has been written about Violette's colleagues.

Of the three women, Denise Madeleine Bloch was the one who had spent the most time in the field. A French woman who spoke English, she was recruited into the Resistance in Lyons by René Piercy, code names *Adolphe* and *Etienne,* in July 1942. She was by profession a secretary and had worked for Jean Maxim Aron, who was an official at the Citröen Works. Jean Maxim Aron was himself a member of the Resistance, using the code name *Joseph.* Denise in turn recruited her fiancé, M. Mendelsohn, for the Resistance.

Denise's first task was to look after a British wireless operator, Brian Stonehouse, code name *Celestin*, who had arrived in France to work with the Detective circuit in the area between Tours and

Poitiers during the month in which she was recruited. Although he spoke good French, his accent betrayed him as an Englishman and Denise accompanied him about the countryside ensuring that his identity was not discovered. He liked to draw and always carried a sketchbook with him, which worried Denise as she thought it was a security risk.

One day towards the end of October Denise was going to meet Stonehouse when she saw him in the street with two other men. She did not acknowledge him but followed the trio and realized when they stopped at the police station that Stonehouse had been arrested. The Frenchman who had been hiding Stonehouse was also arrested and Denise believed that they had both been shot. She was wrong about Stonehouse as he survived not only this arrest but also the war.

A day or so after his arrest Denise went to Marseilles and from there accompanied Jean Maxim Aron and another Resistance member, Henri Sevenet, code name *Rodolphe,* to Lyons. When they arrived at the station at Lyons the Gestapo were waiting for them and arrested Jean Aron. By sheer luck Denise had taken another exit from the station and emerged into the street unnoticed. Henri Sevenet also escaped.

It seems that Denise may have been the reason for the arrest of Jean Aron as she had sent a telegram to her mother telling her when she would be returning to Lyons. The Gestapo had intercepted the message and were waiting at the station. Denise found that they had been to Aron's flat and had found photos of him with his family, so knew who to look for, but they did not know what she looked like which is how she managed to escape. Shortly afterwards they raided the flat of her fiancé, M. Mendelsohn, arrested him and removed a number of pictures of her. She knew that she had to escape and so hid herself away for a few days at St Laurent de Chamousset near Lyons. On 10 November she went to Villefranche-sur-Mer where she stayed until 2 January 1943 not working at all and hardly daring to go out except to have her hair dyed blonde in an attempt to disguise herself.

By mid-January Henri Sevenet came to see her and told her that it was too dangerous for her to remain in France. He took her to Toulouse where he introduced her to Yvon Dupont, code name *Abelard*, who was later to become the organizer for the Diplomat circuit. He agreed to take her to Oloron so that she could cross over the Pyrenees into Spain. They made the journey by bus but when they arrived they found that it had been snowing so heavily that it was impossible for Denise to cross the mountains.

She returned to Toulouse where she met Colonel George Starr, code name *Hilaire*, who took her to work for him in his Wheelwright circuit near the town of Agen. While she was there Denise lived under the name of Katrine Bernard, but also obtained a second set of papers in the name of Chantal Baron. When the organizer of the neighbouring Prunus circuit, Lieutenant Maurice Pertschuk, code name *Eugene*, and his radio operator, Lieutenant Marcus Bloom, code name *Urbain*, were arrested in April 1943, George Starr decided to send Denise to London with a full report. She was again accompanied by Dupont, who was being sent to London for training, and this time they managed to get through.

Leaving Agen on 29 April they went first to Toulouse, then on to Montrejeau where they spent the night. The next day they spent three hours on a train, crossing seventeen kilometres of the *zone interdite* to get to Cirs de Luchon, where they were directed to the Hotel des Trois Ormeaux by the *chef de gare*. The proprietor of the hotel, who believed that Denise was English, gave them a room and they waited there while he found two guides to take them through the mountains and on into Spain.

Just after midnight they left the hotel and began the long walk. It was still extremely cold up in the mountains with a lot of snow on the ground. Denise was wearing a jacket and had bare legs and thin shoes. They walked for many hours through the snow until at about 3 p.m. they reached the town of Bausen. One of the guides stayed with Denise while the other went on ahead into the town to make sure that it was safe for her and Yvon to be there. Denise was so cold that the guide made a fire to warm her. She paid one of them 3000 francs and the other 2000 francs, but believed that they would have helped her anyway, even if she hadn't had any money.

They arrived in Bausen on a Saturday and just missed the bus, so had to wait for the next one which was due on the following Monday. After the long and difficult walk both Denise and Yvon were glad of the rest. On Monday the bus arrived and they boarded it without any problems. They went on to Veille and then to Lerida, where Denise bumped into the British Consul who was taking a short break from his duties in Barcelona. She had dinner with him that night and he arranged papers which would allow her and Yvon to go directly to Madrid.

They arrived in Madrid on 8 May and remained there for five days while the onward trip to Gibraltar was arranged. They reached Gibraltar on Saturday, 15 May and stayed for three more days before going on to London via Lisbon, arriving on 21 May. The trip had taken twenty-two days from start to finish.

Once in London Denise was commissioned into the FANY with the rank of Ensign and was sent to STS52 at Thame Park in the small Oxfordshire town of Thame. For the next ten months she was trained to be a wireless operator. After a brief spell of parachute training at Ringway, Denise was given the code name *Ambroise* and was sent back to France. She went by Lysander on the night of 2 March 1944 and was accompanied by a Frenchman, pre-war world champion racing driver Robert Benoist, code name *Lionel*, organizer of the Clergyman circuit, in the Nantes region of western France. Denise was to be his wireless operator. The Lysander was piloted by Flight Lieutenant M. Anderson of 161 Squadron and landed in a field ten kilometres south of the town of Vatan, in the département of Indre, from where the pair took a train to Nantes.

Benoist was returning to France to resurrect the Clergyman circuit and, with the build up to D-Day, there was much work to be done. The instructions were to blow up pylons across the Loire River at Ile Heron and to train groups to cut railway lines in and out of Nantes and to cut telephone lines. These tasks required the formation of groups of men who had to be trained and supplied in the short time between their arrival in March and D-Day. Of course they were not certain when D-Day would be, but they knew they had a lot of work to do to ensure they were ready when it did arrive and, in fact, they had only three months before the Allied forces began streaming back into Europe.

Two weeks after arriving back in France Denise made her first successful contact with London and went on to send thirty-one messages in the three months that she was active and to receive fifty-two. Tragedy struck on 18 June while Robert Benoist was visiting his dying mother in Paris. The Gestapo arrested him as he went to see his mother and he was sent to Buchenwald concentration camp. The following day other members of the circuit, including racing driver Jean-Paul Wimille's wife and Denise who had been waiting for Benoist at the Villa Cecile at Sermaise, were also arrested. Denise was taken to Fresnes and then on to Saarbrücken and to Ravensbrück.

Violette's other companion during the last months of her life was Lilian Vera Rolfe. She and her twin sister, Helen Fedora, were born at 32 avenue Duquesne in Paris on 26 April 1914 and were baptised at the British Embassy Church in Paris on 7 July 1916.

Avenue Duquesne is a pleasant, wide, tree-lined avenue. Its buildings are tall and elegant, with shutters to the windows and wrought-iron balconies, and it is full of history. At one end is the *Ecole Militaire*, the military academy, founded by King Louis XV, where Napoleon was trained. On the other side, just a few streets away, is the magnificent golden dome of the *Eglise du Dôme* at *Les Invalides*, the military hospital founded by King Louis XIV and the final resting place of Napoleon, whose body was returned to Paris from St Helena nineteen years after his death. Add to this a view of the Eiffel Tower and you have a picture of the sights that surrounded Lilian Rolfe during her childhood.

Her father, George Rolfe, a chartered accountant, was a Londoner. Coincidentally Lilian, like Violette, had links with the Brixton and Stockwell area of London. Her father had once lived in Knatchbull Road, Brixton, and her grandparents lived in nearby Paulet Road.

When Lilian and Helen were about sixteen years old the family moved from Paris to Rio de Janeiro in Brazil. Lilian went to work at the Canadian legation and at the British embassy in Rio and was there at the outbreak of the war.

By 1943 she had decided that she wanted to do more than stay in the comparative safety of South America and so she and her friend Cynthia Sadler boarded a ship bound for England. After a hazardous journey, which took them to the United States after their ship was attacked, they eventually arrived in England where they both joined the WAAF. On 16 April 1943 Lilian became 2149745 Aircraftwoman Second Class Rolfe and began her training as a wireless operator. A WAAF clerk may have incorrectly noted Lilian's personal details as, after she enlisted, she was always known as Lilian Verna Rolfe and not Lilian Vera.

When it became known that Lilian was a fluent French speaker she was approached and asked if she would be willing to 'volunteer for special duties'. This she did and on 26 November 1943 was accepted into SOE as a wireless operator. She was sent to STS52 at Thame Park on 1 January 1944 and remained there until 22 March when she successfully completed her course. Her instructors reported that she was very good at coding and 'steady with her Morse', but that she was less good at handling the wireless equipment, although she did improve with practice. She was described as being highly intelligent, sensitive, shy, reticent, painstaking and idealistic.

When her training was complete she was given her code name *Nadine* and the false identity of Claude Irene Rodier and on 5 April 1944 was flown to France by Lysander, to be the wireless operator for George Wilkinson, code name *Etienne*, and his Historian circuit, which was based near Orléans in the département of Loiret. There is some doubt as to where she was taken that evening. A number of flights were sent out on the night of 5–6 April, among them the Liberator that took Violette Szabo on her first mission. A Lysander from 161 Squadron at Tempsford, piloted by Flight Lieutenant W. Taylor, took agents to a field near Azay-sur-Cher south-east of Tours, while the 161 Squadron diary notes that another Lysander, piloted by Lieutenant Per Hysing-Dahl of the Royal Norwegian Air Force, took three agents to a field near Baudreville, east of Chartres. The latter would have been much closer to the area in which Historian operated, but the operational record of the flight states that Lieutenant Hysing-Dahl went out to France empty and only brought agents back to England that night.

It took Lilian nearly a month to meet up with George Wilkinson and she finally managed to contact him on 2 June 1944, just four days before the Allied landings on the Normandy beaches. Once they had established contact, however, Lilian was kept extremely busy. She was in touch with London on an almost daily basis, sending a total of sixty-seven messages, which allowed the maquis in the département of Loiret to be supplied with arms and ammunition at this vital time. Those in London who received Lilian's messages commented on her consistent accuracy despite the difficult conditions in which she had to operate. The Historian area was swarming with Gestapo at the beginning of June 1944 and Lilian had to keep moving about to avoid discovery.

George Wilkinson was arrested near Orléans at the end of June and was sent to Saarbrücken and then on to the concentration camp of Buchenwald near Weimar. He was in the party that included Robert Benoist, organizer of the Clergyman circuit, of which Denise Bloch was the wireless operator. On 24 August 1944 Allied bombers mounted a raid on an armament factory close to the camp. The SS barracks was also hit and about eighty SS soldiers were killed, with many more injured. In retaliation for the raid the Commandant of Buchenwald ordered the execution of twenty-eight British and French prisoners. On 9 September sixteen prisoners, including Robert Benoist, were hanged. They were strung up on hooks on the wall of the crematorium and slowly strangled. These were followed on 4 October by the other twelve, which included George Wilkinson.

Lilian managed to retain her freedom for another month after Wilkinson's capture. She continued her work, assisting Pierre Charie who took over the Historian circuit following Wilkinson's arrest. At the beginning of July she took part in what was described as 'an engagement with enemy troops' near to Olivet on the south-west outskirts of Orléans. Then on 31 July, while staying at a house in Nangis, she was arrested. The Germans who stormed the house and arrested her were actually looking for someone else. They had not known that Lilian was there and finding her was an unexpected bonus for them.

Lilian was sent to Fresnes prison outside Paris and from there she took the same route as Violette to Saarbrücken and onwards to her death at Ravensbrück.

Chapter Ten

The Women's Camp at Ravensbrück

For *SS Reichsführer* Heinrich Himmler Ravensbrück concentration camp was a goldmine. Located fifty miles north of Berlin near to Lake Fürstenberg, it occupied land reputedly owned by Himmler or by a company of which he was the main shareholder. It is likely that he also profited from the labour of the inmates of the camp and, as chief of police, was able to ensure a constant supply of that labour. It was the only camp built specifically for women but did house a small number of male inmates.

The camp was built prior to the start of the Second World War. In late 1938 500 prisoners were sent from Sachsenhausen to build fourteen barrack blocks, a hospital block known as the Revier, a kitchen and a small separate section to house the men the Germans planned to transfer there. A high wall surrounded the camp, topped by electrified barbed wire. Inside this wall was another inner wall, built to ensure that there would be no attempts at escape.

Ravensbrück was opened in May 1939 when 860 German female prisoners and seven Austrian women arrived from Lichtenburg. With them came the Camp Commandant, *SS Hauptsturmführer* Max Kögel, who was to remain in charge until 1942 when he was transferred to Mauthausen. He was replaced by *SS Hauptsturmführer* Fritz Sühren who was still Commandant when, at the end of April 1945, the Russians liberated the camp.

* * *

In 1939 Himmler had handed over responsibility for the administration and supply of the *Waffen SS* to *Gruppenführer* Oswald Pohl. The control of concentration and labour camps was part of his remit. He organized four main supply companies, one of which, the *Gesellschaft für Textil und Lederverwertung GmbH* (Society for Exploitation of Textile and Leather Work Ltd), was based at Ravensbrück. It was this organization which produced the uniforms for the *Waffen SS* and by the middle of the war its turnover was said to be over nine million marks. Companies such as BMW, Heinkel, Krupp and Siemens all used labour from Ravensbrück, or one of its satellite camps, in their factories. The average cost to these companies was six marks per prisoner per day; from this amount approximately seventy pfennigs was deducted by the camp authorities as being the cost of feeding and clothing the prisoner, leaving a profit of five marks and thirty pfennigs. The only additional expense was the two marks it cost to cremate a body after the prisoner had been worked, and starved, to death.

Ravensbrück was originally built to house 6000 prisoners but that figure increased dramatically and the camp was enlarged four times during the course of the war. By the time Violette Szabo arrived in the late summer of 1944 the number of prisoners was thought to be around 80,000. Towards the end of 1944 another, smaller camp was built a few hundred yards away from the main camp. This was called Uckermark and was the *Jugendlager* (youth camp). It was built to house juvenile prisoners but became known as a convalescent camp. Sick prisoners were selected by the Ravensbrück camp doctors and put in trucks and vans to be transported the short distance to the *Jugendlager*. Sometimes they were taken there, but on other occasions they were put in transport that had been converted to mobile gas chambers and they died of carbon monoxide poisoning from the exhaust fumes of the vehicle itself. The prisoners who did find themselves in the 'convalescent camp' fared no better. A hospital had been set up there and for the first few days, presumably to inspire confidence in the inmates, it was served by a French doctor who was also a prisoner. However, he was soon removed and was replaced by a female guard, Vera Salveguart, and two orderlies, Rapp and Köhler. Salveguart's task was to give poison to the prisoners. The orderlies' only function was to beat to death any who refused to take the poison. Some prisoners who escaped this treatment were made to stand outside in the cold until they died from exposure. This lingering form of execution was apparently used to speed up the mass extermination with which the other facilities could not cope.

The area surrounding Ravensbrück was beautiful, with huge areas of sandy soil covered with pine trees. The crackling underfoot of the pine needles vied with the sound of the gently lapping waters of Lake Fürstenberg and the squawking of the ravens as they swooped and dived overhead. The air had the fresh, clean smell of pine resin. The camp was built just beyond the shores of the lake, its western wall facing the water. The local station was about a mile away and the walk up to the camp was along the shores of the lake, passing some large, elegant villas on the way. But at the gate of the camp the beauty disappeared and ugliness and deprivation became a reality.

Beyond the entrance was an iron barrier set into the inner wall and flanked on either side by green buildings guarded by armed soldiers. In the early years of the camp new arrivals were made to wait in huts with no room to sit or lie down and with very few toilet facilities and no drinking water. If they had brought any food with them this was immediately confiscated. They were given showers and had their heads shaved to prevent the spread of lice. For the next forty days they were kept in quarantine huts, emerging only twice a day for roll call. By the time that Violette and her companions arrived at Ravensbrück, quarantine had been dispensed with, as the camp had far too many inmates to make it a practical procedure. In any case, since the straw mattresses provided in the huts were full of lice, quarantine was a rather pointless exercise.

New prisoners had to learn a different vocabulary to understand the workings and organization of the camp. The new arrivals themselves were known as *Zugangenen* and the Germans referred to a prisoner as a *Stück* or piece. *Aufseherinnen* were the German overseers or guards and the *Oberaufseherin* was the supervisor in charge of the overseers. There were a number of different categories of prisoner, each identified by different coloured patches on their arms. A green triangle identified a common criminal and it was these prisoners who were used as camp policewomen; the *Blockova* or *Blockälteste* was the prisoner in each block appointed to oversee what went on there and she was assisted by at least two *Stubovas* or *Stubältesten.* These prisoners were often as cruel and harsh in their treatment of the other prisoners as the camp authorities themselves.

Women with red triangles on their arms were political prisoners of all nationalities, including Germans. Most of these Germans were referred to as *Bettpolitik as* they had been imprisoned for having sexual relations with foreigners, considered by the state to be unsuitable. *Bettpolitik* were not to be confused with *Asociales* who were actually prostitutes and wore black triangles, as did gypsies and others considered as being racially inferior. Jews wore yellow stars and women accused of having sex with non-Aryans wore yellow and red stars. There were a number of prisoners who wore purple triangles, which denoted imprisonment because of a particular religious belief. These included Jehovah's Witnesses of whom there were approximately 2000 at Ravensbrück. They were known as *Bibelforscherinnen.* Although they did not have an easy time in Ravensbrück, the *Bibelforscherinnen* were at least allowed to go outside the camp sometimes to work in the houses and gardens of the SS personnel, and those that remained inside worked in the laundry or as secretaries in the offices.

One of the most hated and feared women in Ravensbrück was *Oberaufseherin* Dorothea Binz, known to the prisoners as 'The Binz'. She was a small blonde woman with a vicious temper who, accompanied by a big dog, used to strut around the camp brandishing a whip, which she frequently used on any prisoner who happened to get in her way. At one time she was in charge of camp floggings, which very few prisoners survived. At the end of the war she was arrested by the British authorities and was sent for trial as a war criminal.

The daily routine of the camp started with a roll call or *appell.* The prisoners were awoken by the sound of a shrill siren at 3 a.m. and had to be dressed and standing outside by 3.45 a.m. Since they only had one thin dress, one pair of knickers and a pair of wooden clogs to wear, this didn't take very long. No one ever undressed, as there was nothing to wear in bed except their day clothes. They lined up in rows of ten under the huge camp searchlights and often had to stand for as long as two hours or more while the count was taken. Any prisoners who tried to evade *appell* were savagely beaten. No one, not even those who were sick or dying, was excused. As the guards approached each block the women were called to attention by the *Blockova* and had to stand with their arms at their sides for as long as it took to be counted. Sometimes the temperature was as low as minus 20 degrees Celsius but the inmates were not even allowed to put their hands in their pockets in a futile effort to keep warm.

When the roll call was complete a second roll call started. This was the labour roll call and took place in the *Lagerstrasse*, the main street of the camp. This was to account for the prisoners who would be working during the morning; a further labour roll call was made at 12.30 p.m. which was for the afternoon work force. The last roll call of the day, which was abolished towards the end of the war, was at 5.30 p.m. when the workers returned after their day's toil. After that the women were allowed to return to their miserable accommodation, which consisted of rows of triple bunks, covered with thin straw mattresses and where the women were crowded in, at least two to each bunk. There were no blankets and they had to huddle together and rely on each other for warmth.

Violette arrived at Ravensbrück sometime between late August and early September 1944. One of the first people she bumped into was Marie Lecomte, 'Maman Marie', her friend from Fresnes. Marie was shocked by Violette's appearance. When they had parted a little more than two weeks before she had looked reasonably well. Now she was thin and worn out. She told Marie that all she wanted to do was sleep. Although it was not permitted to enter the huts during the day, Marie told Violette to climb in through the window of her own hut and to take a top bunk. She said that she would wake her in time for roll call. Violette gratefully scrambled in through the window and slept until the evening roll call. They then stayed together talking about what had happened to each of them since they had been together in Fresnes.

Unlike Violette, Marie had come directly to Ravensbrück from

Fresnes, which she had left only a few days after Violette. She was shocked to hear about the treatment given to Violette and her companions and saw the marks on her ankle and wrist made by the iron weight and the chains. She also heard about the terrible food, which seemed to be even worse than that served in Ravensbrück.

After she had been at Ravensbrück for a few days Violette also met up with a French girl that she knew, who had worked with the Resistance. I will call her Hélène, although that is not her real name. Although she was happy to tell me her story she didn't want her true identity to be revealed.

Hélène saw Violette, Denise and Lilian soon after their arrival at Ravensbrück, but also saw that the presence of British women had attracted a lot of attention. She had suffered greatly at the hands of the Gestapo and was anxious not to draw attention to herself in any way, not wanting to go through any more suffering. However, after a few days she realized that by staying apart from this group she was, in fact, making herself conspicuous and so she plucked up the courage to speak to the British girls. Violette was delighted to see her again, although sad at the circumstances of the meeting. She asked Hélène how she had been treated and was shocked to learn that she had been subjected to the treatment of the *baignoire*, a bath of cold water under which her head had been held repeatedly until she almost lost consciousness. Violette said that she herself had not been treated badly at all, apart from the chains around her wrist and ankle on the journey from Fresnes. It would seem from what I have been told that French women were sometimes subjected to torture, but that British women, although badly treated, were not actually tortured. This may account for Odette Churchill's claim that she had been tortured. Although she worked with SOE she was, in fact, French.

Hélène recalled that during those first days at Ravensbrück Violette's mind was full of plans to escape. She was the liveliest of the three British girls; Denise was very depressed and Lilian, although mentally quite strong, had been weakened by illness and had to be helped by the others. Violette wanted Hélène to escape with her but before they had the chance to make any firm plans they were all sent to Torgau to work in the munitions factory. Torgau lies approximately seventy-five miles south of Berlin on the River Elbe. It was here on 25 April 1945 that the conquering armies of the Allies and the Soviet Union finally met, amid scenes of jubilation. According to one eyewitness, 'It was like the finale of a circus'. However, at the time Violette was there Torgau was far less appealing.

Marie was also in the group sent to Torgau, but she fell ill during the train journey and, on arrival, was taken to the camp hospital. Violette visited her there and talked to her, but Marie was so ill she didn't recognize her. Everyone thought she would die; she was semi-conscious and bleeding from her mouth, but her sense of survival was strong and she eventually recovered, both physically and mentally.

Violette met up with Hélène again and they began to plan their escape. There were a number of gates in the fence around the camp and Violette decided she would try to get a key made that would allow them to go through the gates. Hélène wanted to take a chance and try to escape immediately, but Violette thought it would be better if they planned it properly. About ten days after they first spoke about escaping, Hélène and Violette met again. Violette had managed to get a key but had had to throw it away as someone had found out about it and had told the authorities. Soon after that the French and the British girls were separated and Hélène was sent to Abteroda, one of the sub-camps of Ravensbrück. She recalled how sad she was at not being able to stay with Violette and said of her:

> She was a very solid person, a tomboy, but very kind. She would have done anything to help anyone else. I would have liked to have gone with her. I never saw her again. I suppose I was lucky, I could have been sent back to Ravensbrück like she was and been executed.

Hélène did finally manage to escape just before the end of the war and, after a difficult and dangerous journey on foot, was eventually repatriated by the Americans.

While Violette and her friends were working in Torgau some trouble started in the camp. One of the women, a communist, began advising the women to stop working on the munitions that would 'kill our Brothers'. No one was sure what to do. The doctor at the camp, an elderly German who had been good to the prisoners, advised them not to be foolish. He told them that they would be wise to stay where they were and work in the munitions factory, where conditions were far superior to those at Ravensbrück. There were 500 women who had been transferred from Ravensbrück to Torgau at that time. Some agreed that it was better to work and at least have conditions that were just about bearable than be sent back to the hellish conditions of Ravensbrück; others agreed with the communist and refused to do any more work. The local camp authorities were unable to handle the situation and so Fritz Sühren, the commandant at Ravensbrück, had to come to Torgau to sort out the mess created by his prisoners. He decided to send 250 of the women to work in a factory in Leipzig. The other 250, which included Violette, Denise, Lilian and Marie, were sent to a harsh work camp at Königsberg in eastern Prussia, 300 miles from Ravensbrück. (Königsberg was absorbed into the USSR at the end of the war and was renamed Kaliningrad.) These 250 women were the ones that were punished for the mutiny, although most of them had no responsibility for it at all. Marie described that day, which was around 19 October 1944, as being the blackest in her life,

The camp had formerly been occupied by Russian prisoners who had left it in a filthy state. The palliasses on which the women slept were full of vermin, the food was terrible and there was very little heating. To make matters worse it was now November and the outside temperature was below freezing.

The women were set to work clearing trees and digging ground that was as hard as iron, so that the Germans could have a new airfield. It was back-breaking work, made much worse by the weather, which had now turned to snow, brought in by the bitter east wind. Marie was the luckiest of the four women. She was feeling unwell and was sent to the medical facility at the camp, such as it was. There she was put in the care of a Corsican doctor named Maria de Perete, who ensured that, for a time at least, she was not sent out on any of the work parties. Instead she was put in charge of distributing the meagre rations allocated to her hut. These consisted of soup made from water and the unwashed peelings from potatoes or beet, and bread; one small loaf had to be shared between fourteen women. If the bread was cut carefully, it was possible for each woman to have two thin slices per day. One day the soup was accidentally spilt and the girls scrambled around on the filthy floor looking for pieces of peeling that they could retrieve and eat, as they knew there would be nothing to replace it.

In a letter written to Violette's parents after the war, Marie Lecomte recalled how, one evening, when Violette arrived back at the hut at about 6 p.m., she was almost out of her mind with the cold. The cheerful, optimistic girl, who, only a short time before had planned to escape, was gone. The girl who replaced her was depressed, exhausted and devoid of any hope for the future. That point must have been one of the lowest in her life. She began to scream and cry and Marie took her in her arms and tried to bring some warmth back to her aching limbs. She kept saying, 'I am so cold, so cold.'

Slowly she became calm again. Marie had saved her a few pieces of potato, which she stuck to the side of the stove to warm. The food seemed to cheer her and soon she was back to something resembling her normal self.

The hard labour and the dreadful weather continued for another month, but there was worse to come. The commandant at Königsberg did not treat the women too badly, but one day he was suddenly replaced. Fritz Sühren arrived from Ravensbrück, bringing with him a woman who was put in charge of the prisoners. She made it her business to make life as unpleasant for the women as she possibly could, beating them with a whip and kicking them with feet clad in heavy boots. Marie, mercifully, escaped this treatment. The doctor had told the commandant that she was 'sick in the head' and so she was left alone for a while. It seems likely that she escaped this cruelty more because the torturer did not expect to get a normal reaction from someone who was mentally disturbed than from any sense of compassion.

One evening Violette arrived back at the hut after having been away for a few days with a work party. She was very cold and climbed onto Marie's bunk, where they hugged each other to get warm. *La commandante*, as Marie referred to the new camp chief, had banned the women from having any heating at all in their huts and the metal stove stood empty and cold. Some of the girls were shivering so badly that they decided they would light a fire anyway, in spite of the rules. Marie tried to reason with them, pointing out what the consequences of their action might be, but they were determined and fetched some wood to start the fire. By 10 p.m. *la commandante* was at the hut demanding to know who had started the fire. No one spoke and she continued to demand an answer, telling the prisoners that if no one owned up they would all be made to spend the night outside in the snow, which would, of course, mean certain death for them all. Still not getting a reply to her question, *la commandante* then wanted to know who was in charge of the hut. Marie said that she was and *la commandante* marched over to her, pushing Violette to one side and slapped Marie's face twice. She demanded to know if she had understood what was being said to her and, although she had Marie replied, 'No, I don't speak German.' In a fury *la commandante* grabbed Marie by the shoulders and pushed her against the stove-pipe, which was, by now, very hot. She received a bad burn but was given no treatment for it and was told to report to *la commandante* the next day. She was made to walk through the snow in her bare feet, which resulted, subsequently, in a bout of pneumonia. When she eventually was allowed to return to her hut she found that each of the girls had saved a spoonful of soup from their own rations for her.

The work continued. Every day Violette, Denise and Lilian were made to cut down trees and clear ground, this time for the roads that would lead in and out of the airfield. Other women had joined them, one of whom became friendly with Violette. Her name was Solange Rousseau and she greatly admired Violette's courage and cheerfulness. Lilian was very sick by now and could hardly do any work at all; Denise was still very depressed and even Violette's spirit had been damaged, but was not entirely crushed. The women moved around like walking skeletons, too weak and undernourished to accomplish much, but still demands were made of them. The only kindness shown to them was during the week they worked with a group of Austrian soldiers, who shared their food with them. Many of the women died where they worked among the trees.

In the letter written by Marie to Violette's parents in the late 1950s she says of that time:

> You will understand why I feel shocked when I see pictures of the film on Violette with the women in the camp wearing so much clothes – my poor darling had only one blue silk frock, a fringe from hem to her knees and short sleeved, this is the way we were clothed to face a Prussian winter.

The old year drew to a close and 1945 began. Around 19 or 20 January an order was received at Königsberg that Violette Szabo, Denise Bloch and Lilian Rolfe were to be returned to Ravensbrück. According to Lilian's friend, Renée Corjon, the order was received at about 10 p.m. and the girls were told to be ready by 5 a.m. the next morning. In preparation for the journey back, the German authorities suddenly decided to show some compassion to the three women and issued them with different clothes, soap and a comb. Violette exchanged her thin blue dress for a blouse, skirt and a coat. She was also given a pair of shoes. Of course, none of the clothing was new, but they, and the soap and comb, brought her great joy. She asked Marie to help her wash her back and remove the lice from her hair. When she had washed herself and her hair, and had put on her new outfit she said that she felt quite decent again.

It did occur to Violette to question why they had been called back to Ravensbrück and why they had been given new clothing. She was uneasy about it and thought it was not a good sign at all. Marie tried to reassure her by saying that the Germans were probably going to move her to a camp with British prisoners and that they would not want the others to see the pitiful state in which she had had to exist. She tried to cheer her up by telling her that from then on she would probably be getting good food to eat and, maybe, even chocolate. Her kind words unfortunately had the opposite effect to that which she intended and Violette promptly burst into tears and flung herself into Marie's arms. She told Marie that she had a premonition that there were only bad things to come and said she wished she could stay at Königsberg with her.

Then she asked Marie to make her a promise. She wanted

reassurance that Marie would go to London to see her mother and father, her brothers and, of course, Tania, if she herself did not survive whatever was in store for her. She wrote her parents' address on a tiny slip of paper, which Marie rolled up and pushed into the hem of her dress. She made Marie repeat the address again and again so she could be sure it wouldn't be forgotten. She then made a promise to Marie that if she did survive and Marie did not, she would look after her family. She told Marie she must not worry, as she would make some money from films and that her family would want for nothing. One wonders how she would have reacted had she been told, at that moment, that thirteen years later a film would be made about her own life and that, more than fifty years on, the name of Violette Szabo would still be remembered.

Marie and Violette hugged each other and looked forward to the time when they would both be free and would be able to visit each other as friends should. When it was time for her to leave, Violette kissed Marie seven times, one kiss for each member of her family, and asked her to tell them what had happened to her during the time they spent together. Then she, Denise and Lilian left the camp for the last time.

When they reached Ravensbrück they were put into solitary confinement where they remained for a few days before being transferred back to the main part of the camp. Those who saw them when they returned to Ravensbrück all commented on the terrible state the three British girls were in, and this was after they had been given soap and a change of clothes. It is hard to imagine how bad they must have looked before this transformation.

It soon became clear to the girls that they were not going to be sent to a prisoner of war camp, nor would they ever again eat decent food or wear pretty clothes. One evening, a few days after their return to Ravensbrück, they were sent for and were taken to a narrow alley between the isolation block and the inner wall. There Fritz Sühren, the camp commandant, read out a statement ordering their execution. One by one the girls were forced to kneel and were shot in the back of the neck by *SS Sturmmann* Schult. Lilian and Denise were said to have been too weak to walk without help but Violette walked to her death unaided. Immediately after the execution their clothes were removed and their bodies cremated. The date of the execution was sometime between 26 January and 5 February 1945. In a statement made by Vera Atkins in March 1946, she says:

> Today I have heard the full story from one of the few eye-witnesses, SS *Obersturmführer* J. Schwarzhüber who held the post of *Schutzhaftlagerführer* (Camp Overseer) in Ravensbrück and who is now under arrest. I attach copies of the translation of a statement which I took from him. In short he states that the girls' names figured on a list drawn up by the Gestapo in Berlin of persons to be executed. They were recalled from the *Aussenkommando* Königsberg to the main camp and shot one evening under arrangements made by the Camp Commandant Sühren (also under arrest). Their bodies were cremated.
>
> Every witness, even the miserable Sühren, has expressed the greatest admiration at the courage and cheerful behaviour of these girls. They suffered most during the winter months at Königsberg where they were employed in severe weather on heavy outdoor work. Lilian's health broke down completely and Denise was very ill. Violette appears to have stood up to it better. The three of them always stood together and showed remarkable spirit in the face of great hardship.

Marie Lecomte remained at Königsberg until 5 February 1945, when she and 250 other women were made to march back to Ravensbrück. She called it a 'death march' and described how small children threw stones at them along the way and beat them with sticks as they wearily trudged through villages on the long route back. The SS guards used to fire machine guns over their heads to make them run. They thought it a great sport and derived much amusement from the suffering they caused to the poor, emaciated creatures they were guarding. Many of the women fell by the side of the road and were left to die where they fell. Of the 250 that left Königsberg only 160 arrived at Ravensbrück, where they were immediately put into a tent and made to spend the first night out in the snow. That night sixty more women died. Then typhus and dysentery broke out and the Germans decided that the remaining women from that long march would have to be exterminated to prevent the spread of disease.

The women were made to stand in a long queue waiting for their turn to go into the gas chamber, which the Nazis had hurriedly built the previous November when it became obvious that their existing methods of mass murder were too slow and inefficient. As she stood in line waiting, Marie spoke to a French prisoner who had been made a camp policewoman. The French woman asked her if she had been at Ravensbrück before and, if so, what was her number? Marie told her the number, 75387, and she wrote it on a piece of white rag and told her to keep it with her and use it. She then indicated the chimney of the crematorium and said that if she didn't show the guards the number that would be where she would go. Whatever the significance of the number was, the ruse worked and Marie was spared the gas chamber. It may have been that the Germans believed she was not part of the group from Königsberg because she had a number that was issued much earlier than those allocated to the group.

When the camp was overrun, she was sent, in a British ambulance, to a hospital in Pilsen and from there she went by plane to Paris for a long spell of treatment and convalescence. When she left Ravensbrück she was given a new dress to wear and, while she was changing into it, her old dress was taken away. With it went the scrap of paper on which Violette had written her parents' address. It took Marie Lecomte thirteen years to find the Bushells, by which time they had moved to Australia.

Prior to the executions of the three girls there were signs that something was about to happen. Rumours spread after some of the prisoners, employed as secretaries or as orderlies in the SS canteen, noticed the telltale signs – urgent meetings between SS personnel, hurried conversations and an extra ration of alcohol for the guards in the canteen. These signs were quickly reported back to the other prisoners.

Germaine Tillion, a French anthropologist and herself a Ravensbrück inmate, described in her book *Ravensbrück, An eyewitness account of a women's concentration camp* the execution of a number of women, three of whom were British and were described as 'little paratroopers'. It is likely that the women to whom she referred were Violette Szabo, Denise Bloch and Lilian Rolfe. She says:

> We managed to reconstruct, step by step, the circumstances of their deaths. There were nine of them, all women: four French, three English, one Czech, and one Russian. They had to leave behind their shoes and part of their clothing, and then left the camp accompanied by an *Aufseherin*, Ruth Neudecker (born Breslau, 1913), later an *Aufseherin* at *Jugendlager*, and always a volunteer for executions. On the way out, their route, which led past the crematorium towards the Siemens factory, was barred by the SS. A few days later their numbered dresses were found in the clothing-storage depot.

It appears that some of the remaining prisoners refused to believe that their comrades had been executed and preferred to think they had merely been transferred to another camp. However, they discovered that the SS had ordered the building of gallows, which seemed to indicate that the 'little paratroopers' had, in fact, been executed. Germaine Tillion goes on to say:

> To our small group at least, the executions could no longer be questioned; we were right, unfortunately, and our conclusions seemed to be supported by the presence of the new gallows. One thought was obvious at the time: our comrades had been hanged. There is little doubt that they were executed, but probably by firearms, or so I believe today.
>
> One year later, in fact, the deputy commandant of Ravensbrück, under questioning by an English judge, gave an account of the executions and declared they had been shot. His statements, to the extent that I could check them, I found to be true.

The gallows had been built not for the execution of the nine women, but for the small group of German officers implicated in the plot to assassinate Hitler on 20 July 1944, who were being held in solitary confinement at Ravensbrück at that time.

* * *

When she first returned to Ravensbrück Marie Lecomte spoke to a French nurse and asked her if she knew what had happened to Violette. She didn't know, but promised to find out and returned sometime later with the news that Violette was dead. Marie was too upset to talk to her at that moment, but sought her out the next day to discover what had happened. She was told that the nurse thought Violette had been hanged. She said that she had seen her clothes in the disinfection room and that there was blood on them. Marie asked her to describe the clothes and recognized them as the ones Violette had been wearing when they were last together. However, as she told the nurse, when a person is hanged there is no blood. In his deposition Johann Schwarzhüber clearly stated that when the girls had been shot, their clothes had been burnt with their bodies. In view of the testimony of both Marie Lecomte and Germaine Tillion, this seems unlikely. Even after death the Germans had allowed them no dignity, stripping them of clothes that were little more than rags, presumably so that they could save a few pfennigs and pass them on to some other poor women.

Chapter Eleven

After the War

All through the second half of 1944 and on into 1945 Mr and Mrs Bushell waited for news of their daughter. They always believed that Violette would come home one day, but as the war drew to a close they began to wonder whether they had been wrong to hope. VE Day came and went and still there was no news of Violette. They contacted anyone they thought might be able to help with news of her, the Red Cross, members of parliament and even newspapers, one or two of which ran stories about the missing girl and showed pathetic little pictures of Tania looking at photos of her mother and supposedly asking the question, 'Where is my mummy?'

Eventually Vera Atkins decided that she must go to Germany and find out what had happened to Violette and to the other agents of SOE who were also still unaccounted for. She uncovered a depressingly large number of tragic stories. Of the women agents alone she discovered that thirteen, including Violette, had not survived imprisonment by the Germans. (The names of these thirteen women can be found at the end of the book in Appendix E.)

Horrific stories emerged of the atrocities committed by the Nazis. Some of the captured agents had survived and came back from the concentration camps with their own stories of ill treatment, hunger and deprivation. They were perhaps the lucky ones, although they have had to live with the memories of that terrible time and with the loss of so many of their friends and colleagues ever since.

Miss Atkins interviewed *SS Obersturmführer* Johann

Schwarzhüber, who was the Deputy Camp Commandant at Ravensbrück, and took from him the following statement.

> I declare that I remember that I had delivered to me towards the end of January 1945 from the German Secret Police an Order countersigned by the Camp Commandant Sühren instructing me to ascertain the location of the following persons: Lilian Rolfe, Danielle Williams *(Denise Bloch was sometimes known as Danielle Williams)* and Violet Szabo.
>
> These were at that time in the dependant camp of Königsberg on the Oder and were recalled by me. When they returned to the camp they were placed in the punishment block and moved from there into the block of cells.
>
> One evening, towards 19.00 hours, they were called out and taken to the courtyard by the crematorium. Camp Commandant Sühren made these arrangements. He read out the order for their shooting in the presence of the Chief Camp Doctor Trommer, SS Sergeant Zappe, SS Lance Corporal Schult or Schulter (a block leader from the men's camp), SS Corporal Schenk (in charge of the Crematorium), dentist Dr Hellinger. I was myself present.
>
> The shooting was done only by Schult with a small calibre gun through the back of the neck. Death was certified by Dr Trommer. The corpses were removed singly by the internees who were employed in the Crematorium and burnt. The clothes were burnt with the bodies.
>
> I accompanied the three women to the Crematorium yard. A female camp overseer was also present and was sent back when we reached the Crematorium. Zappe stood guard over them while they were waiting to be shot.
>
> All three were very brave and I was deeply moved. Sühren was also impressed by the bearing of these women. He was annoyed that the Gestapo did not themselves carry out these shootings.
>
> I recognize with certainty the photograph of Danielle Williams and I think I recognize the photograph of Lilian Rolfe. I know that the third had the name of Violette.

I am prepared to make this declaration under oath.

Read, found correct and signed of my own free will.

(signed) Johann Schwarzhüber

Signed before me this thirteenth day of March, 1946 at Tomato, Minden

(signed) V. M. Atkins

Squadron Officer.

In December 1946 the accused of Ravensbrück were sent for trial for their war crimes. SOE advisor Duncan Stuart let me have the following account of the proceedings:

On 5 December 1946, a British Military Court in Hamburg, under the presidency of Major-General P. Westropp, CB CBE, began hearing the charges against the accused of Ravensbrück. There were thirteen members of the prison staff and three former prisoners.

Camp Commandant Sühren had escaped from prison and was still at large. Commandant Kögel had already committed suicide earlier in the year.

The Court was advised by the Deputy Judge-Advocate General and consisted of a further five British officers, one French and one Polish judge. The prosecution team was led by Major Steven Stuart, with Captain John da Cunha, Madame Chalufour a French advocate and Squadron Officer Vera Atkins of F Section, SOE. Witnesses were French, Belgian, Dutch, Danish, Norwegian, Austrian, Polish, Czech, Swiss and German. The immense problem of translating from all these languages was undertaken with distinction by a team under Major Peter Forest.

The Court heard evidence that many more than 100,000 women had been sent to Ravensbrück. It held around 12,000 at any one time. The harshness of the conditions, the brutal punishment and neglect accounted for a death rate of almost 100% per year. Conditions were even worse in hospital where women were left to die or be subjected to lethal experiments. At the beginning of 1945, Himmler ordered that those ill or incapable of marching were to be killed. Mass slaughter began. When 200 were being shot each day, Sühren complained it was not fast enough. A gas chamber was built where nearly 24,000 women were gassed, 150 at a time. Others were dragged alive into the crematorium.

Before the sentencing, one defendant, Dr Winkelman, who had selected women for the gas chamber, died from a stroke. On 3 February 1947 all remaining defendants were found guilty. They were sentenced as follows:

Sentenced to Death

Carmen Mory	Block Leader, Collaborator
Vera Salveguart	Nurse, Extermination Camp
Dorothea Binz	Chief Wardress, punishment block
Elizabeth Marschall	Hospital Matron
Greta Boesel	Head of Labour Gang
Johann Schwarzhüber	Deputy Camp Commandant
Rolf Rosenthal	Assistant Doctor
Gustav Binder	Labour Gang Leader
Percy Treite	Deputy Chief Medical Officer
Ludwig Ramdohr	Interrogator, Chief of Security
Doctor Schidlausky	Chief Medical Officer

15 Years Imprisonment

Captain Peters	Commander of Camp Guard
Doctor Hellinger	Dentist

10 Years Imprisonment

Eugenia von Skene	Collaborator
Margaret Mewes	Bunker Wardress

Camp Commandant Sühren was eventually tried and executed in 1950.

Vera Atkins' discovery was the end of all hope for the Bushell family, who had to come to terms with the fact that Violette was dead. It may not have been a consolation to them at the time but at least Violette's death, by a shot in the neck, had been instant. The end for some of the others had not been as merciful. Eyewitnesses to the execution of the four women in the camp at Natzweiler have stated that at least two of the women were alive when they were put into the fire at the crematorium and that one of them was still conscious, following what was supposed to be a lethal injection. A German guard watched in horror as the hair of one of the women caught fire even before the door to the oven was closed. Having to watch this obscenity was the final straw for this man. He vomited on the floor and then ran from the scene and didn't stop running until he was well away from the camp. I was told this by the person who later interrogated him and have been unable to wipe the image from my mind. I can't begin to understand how the perpetrators of these crimes managed to live with themselves, knowing what they had done, and yet some of them were proud of their actions and remained defiant to the end. Tragically, this particular incident was not unique.

In 1945 the first electoral register since before the war was made. While I was doing my research someone sent me a copy of the 1945 register and those for the years 1946 to 1949 for Pembridge Villas in Notting Hill. I was astonished to find the name Violette R.E. Szabo listed on each register from 1945 to 1948. I telephoned the Kensington and Chelsea council offices to ask how their colleagues would have made the register in 1945 and was told that, as there were no electoral registers made during the war years, the first post-war register in 1945 would have been made from the last pre-war register in 1939. I asked how it was possible to include the name of a person who in 1939 lived in another district and was, in any case, too young to vote. I was told that she must have made a point of registering herself in time for the list of 1945. When I pointed out that she was on all the subsequent lists up to and including 1948 and that she had been executed in January 1945 no one knew what to say. They could give me no explanation whatever as to why this had happened. I asked the SOE advisor at the Foreign and Commonwealth Office if it was likely that someone from SOE had registered her in 1945 in the hope that she might still be alive. He told me that it was not likely and that in any case Vera Atkins had been asked to pay the rent for the flat to Mrs Bushell from Violette's salary at the end of May 1944 and that after that no more rent was paid. It appears that when she knew she was going to make her second trip to France she gave up the flat in Notting Hill. Perhaps Mme Meunier was right when she said that Violette did not intend to come back. The question of the electoral registers remains unanswered.

Violette's parents had brought Tania back from Mill Hill to live with them in Burnley Road, Stockwell, at the end of the war. Having known no other parents, she grew up calling them Mum and Dad.

On 17 December 1946 the citation for the award of the George Cross appeared in the *London Gazette*. The details were not correct and one wonders where the authorities obtained such an inaccurate account. However, Violette had been given one of the highest awards that her country could offer and in January 1947 Mr and Mrs Bushell took Tania to Buckingham Palace to receive the medal. For some days she had been practising her curtsies for the occasion, or 'skirtsies' as she called them. King George VI, when he gave the medal to Tania, is supposed to have told her to take great care of it as it was for her mother.

Outside the Palace photographers took pictures of Tania holding the medal. The last line in the book *Carve Her Name With Pride* tells how Tania is supposed to have said, 'It's for Mummy. I'll keep it for her till she comes home.' It provided a good ending to the book and was designed, no doubt, to tug at the heartstrings of the readers. But it was simply not true. Tania herself told me that her grandparents had explained to her what had happened to her mother and she knew very well that Violette was dead and would never be coming home.

Although Violette had been awarded the Croix de Guerre in September 1944 while in Ravensbrück, there had never been a medal presented to her. This omission was remedied when the French Ambassador René Massigli, who had himself escaped from France on an SOE flight, presented the medal to Tania. Wearing both her mother's and her father's medals was almost too much for the little girl. Etienne had been awarded the Légion d'Honneur, the Médaille Militaire and the Croix de Guerre with Star and Palm and he and Violette were believed to have been the most highly decorated married couple of the entire war. The combined weight of the medals was too much for Tania to carry without some help. Her grandmother had to make her a little harness with straps around her neck and back in order for her to wear all the medals at once.

Violette's colleagues Bob Maloubier and Jean Claude Guiet from the Salesman circuit both survived the war. Jean Claude went back to America where he still lives. After spending some time abroad Bob eventually settled just outside Paris.

Jacques Dufour enlisted in the French Army in 1945 and was sent to Indo-China to fight the communists. In 1946, during a battle with Viet Minh rebels, he was killed.

Philippe Liewer was also killed only a few years after the end of the war. There is some confusion as to what actually happened to him. Some reports say he was killed in an accident in Canada while others report that the accident happened in Casablanca in Morocco. The latter would seem to be most likely as he was living in Morocco and working for a company at 259 boulevard de la Gare in Casablanca. He was last heard from in the spring of 1948 and is presumed to have died soon after.

After the war the French paid tribute to the heroes of Bir Hakeim by changing the name of the Pont de Grenelle, over the Seine in Paris, to the Pont de Bir Hakeim. The nearby Métro station in the boulevard de Grenelle is also named after the desolate outpost that claimed the lives of so many of the Légion Etrangère.

Charles de Gaulle became President of France in the autumn of 1945, resigning three months later. In January 1959 he was again voted into his country's highest office. There were four unsuccessful attempts on his life during his time as President and in 1969 he resigned again following a defeat in a referendum on constitutional change. In spite of the hospitality shown to him by Britain during the war he made no secret of his dislike of it and its people. For the remainder of his life he never lost an opportunity to revile the country that had given him a safe haven during the dark days of the German occupation of France. He died in 1970.

Marie-Pierre Koenig also died in 1970 and four years later was honoured by having a Paris Square named after him. He was posthumously given the rank of Field Marshal.

Maurice Buckmaster, head of F Section, died in 1992, defending to the end both his agents and the decisions he made regarding them. His assistant, the redoubtable Vera Atkins, died on 24 June 2000 at the age of ninety-two. She retained her civilian status until after the war when she joined the WAAF and became a section officer. Photos taken of her at the time show her in uniform and she is often wrongly thought to have been in uniform throughout the war. Her tenacity in the hunting down of war criminals ensured that many of the Nazis who committed atrocities against SOE agents were ultimately brought to justice. She devoted the rest of her life to perpetuating the memory of those who had died for their country and for freedom. At the age of eighty-seven she was created a Commandant of the Légion d'Honneur by the then French President, François Mitterand.

Leo Marks, SOE's brilliant code master lived until January 2001, finally succumbing to cancer.

When all the fuss over the medals had subsided Mr and Mrs Bushell and Tania had to get on with their lives. In the late 1940s Mr Bushell found himself a job as a driver at the atomic weapons research centre at Harwell and the family moved to a house in Wantage.

Violette's brother, Noel, who had been stationed with the Pacific fleet in Sydney during the war, had persuaded his brothers that they would have a better life in Australia and eventually, in the early 1950s, the entire family moved to Australia where Mr and Mrs Bushell and Tania settled in a little place called Long Jetty in New South Wales. Mr Bushell found a job in Sydney, working again for the Rotax company as he had during the war. He lived in a bed-sitter during the week, returning home to Long Jetty at the weekend. It was not an ideal situation, but accommodation was hard to find in Sydney and they did not manage to get a flat together until January 1960, when they rented a flat in the Sydney suburb of Arncliffe. As soon as she was old enough

Tania went as a boarder to St Ursula's College in Armidale in NSW, in the northern part of the mountains of the Great Dividing Range.

In the early 1950s author Rubeigh J. Minney decided to write a biography of Violette and contacted Mr and Mrs Bushell to ask for their help. They were happy to assist in any way they could and eventually *Carve Her Name With Pride* was published in 1956. Soon after its publication they were again approached, this time by a film company, the Rank Organization, who were going to make a film from the book. It was to be directed by Lewis Gilbert and produced by Daniel M. Angel.

Around this time an article about Violette appeared in the Rotax staff magazine, *Reflections*. An employee of the company in England had written it and over the next few years he and Charles Bushell became the best of friends by post. I have been lucky enough to have seen the letters written by Violette's father as the recipient, Douglas Pigg, was the uncle of one of my friends. In one of his first letters, Charles Bushell described the article as being, 'a great tribute to our lost darling Violette'.

At first the letters were full of the proposed film. Mr Bushell was looking forward to returning to England for the première and told his new friend that they would certainly be able to meet for the first time then, as the film company wanted Tania to be there for the opening and were going to arrange for them all to attend. The producer, Daniel Angel, had sent a copy of the script out to Australia and had asked for any comments and suggestions that Mr and Mrs Bushell could offer to be sent back to him. Mr Bushell was happy to make one or two amendments and to correct a couple of errors. He had been unwell; he had had bronchitis, and told Doug:

> all I want is to keep my health and strength so that I shall see the film – that – of course is the greatest thing that could happen to either of us.

Norman Lucas, Charles Bushell's nephew, told me a little story that perhaps explains what appear to have been his uncle's constant bouts of bronchitis. Apparently Mr Bushell smoked Ardath cigarettes and used to claim that he only smoked one cigarette each day. According to his nephew it would have been more correct to say that he only used one match each day as he was a chain smoker, lighting each new cigarette from the butt of the one he was about to stub out.

In the late spring of 1957 came the news that filming was due to start at Pinewood studios and in Burnley Road, Stockwell in July and that the part of Violette had been given to the actress Virginia McKenna. At this point it was obvious that Mr Bushell had no idea who she was. He told Doug that Mrs Bushell was very pleased with the casting, as she had seen Virginia McKenna in *A Town Like Alice* and, 'thinks she is a wonderful actress'. He went on to say that his wife was a very good judge and that, after reading the script, he thought that the film would be the picture of the year and that Virginia McKenna would become a star after it was shown.

For the next few months the letters spoke of nothing but the première and the Bushells' visit to England. By August Mr Bushell was less confident of being able to attend the première. He wrote:

> So far, although we hear from Major Angel from time to time regarding the film, nothing further has been mentioned about our coming over and I am not now as optimistic as I was. It will be a cruel blow to us if we cannot do so, for I can truly say that it is something we have looked forward to for so long. If we cannot come over it will go a long way towards breaking my wife's heart and, as regards myself, although I seem to have been taking some pretty hard knocks all my life, this will be about the hardest blow I shall have taken. To my mind it is, or should be, possible to let Violette's parents be present to view a picture that will be to us a reincarnation of one we loved and are so proud of.

At the beginning of February 1958 Charles Bushell wrote to his friend Doug and, in answer to an enquiry about the film, said:

> No, old man, we have, as yet, heard no word about the 'première' but I have just written to Major Angel, the producer, asking him to let us know when it is coming off.

Then on 23 February he sent another letter, which said:

> Many thanks for your letter received on Thursday 20th. I received a great shock, indeed Mrs Bushell also; we were dismayed to read of the film being shown. It was the first word we had heard about it. I cannot tell you our feelings on the matter, it seems to both of us that we have been treated as outsiders, but many things are involved and the big thing is money.
>
> Would you Doug, please send us a few cuttings of the critics' opinions of the picture?
>
> I cannot say much in this letter as my feelings and thoughts feel numb. My wife wishes to say that she thanks you from the bottom of her heart for your letter. We would rather have heard the bad news from you than anybody.

In the little box of treasures, left to my friend when her uncle and his wife died, was a press cutting about the première of the film *Carve Her Name With Pride*. Although the producer had not considered Mr and Mrs Bushell or Tania important enough to bother with, the guest list was quite impressive. In the audience were Colonel Maurice Buckmaster, head of F Section of SOE; Commander Gerald Holdsworth, the then chairman of the Special Forces Club; the French ambassador, M. Chauvel and Mme Chauvel; Mr and Mrs Geoffrey Hallowes – Mrs Hallowes was the former Odette Churchill, herself an agent, a prisoner in Ravensbrück and holder of the George Cross; Mrs Nancy Forward, the Australian former agent, Nancy Wake; Major Catriona Fernandez, the technical adviser on the film; Sir David Eccles and Lord and Lady Brabourne.

A month after the première had taken place Daniel Angel eventually found the time to inform Violette's family about it and to send them some press cuttings. But Mr Bushell remained upset about the lack of consideration shown to the family and told his friend Doug:

> After all, there could have been no story with its intimate details etc., had it not been for us. Anyway, we are the proud mother and father of one of the world's finest heroines, who

> gave her life in a just cause and that, in itself, is a wonderful thing for us in the few years we have left.

When the film eventually reached Australia in October 1958 the family was again treated with complete disregard. Tania had been promised a private showing before the first night, but that never materialized. Two of Violette's four brothers travelled 700 miles from their homes in Queensland to be at the first performance of the film and, having been told that there was to be an Australian première, at which the family would be the guests of honour, they all went to the trouble and expense of buying evening dress for the occasion only to find that there was no première and that the film had already been shown three times during the day, before the evening performance they were to attend. No one from the film company was present and they were not even greeted by the manager of the State Theatre in Sydney where the film was shown. Interviewed by the press afterwards, Mr Bushell was furious when he read in the subsequent article that he was supposed to have said that the family wished to see the film as ordinary members of the public and angrily retorted:

> This is a complete fabrication. We actually stated that we had been promised a première, and as there was one in London and Paris, there should have been one in Australia, where Violette's daughter, her parents and brothers live. We can only suppose that this report, before being published, was vetted by the powers-that-be at the State Theatre.

A few weeks after the shock of finding out that *Carve Her Name With Pride* had been shown in London without their knowledge, the Bushells received another shock by post. It was the letter from Marie Lecomte, which told them of the promise made by her to Violette when they were together in Ravensbrück.

Marie Lecomte told of how she had tried for nearly thirteen years to contact Mr and Mrs Bushell to fulfil the promise she had made to their daughter. She described how she had been in very poor health following her return from Ravensbrück and how her doctor had urged her to forget the past and try to regain her strength. She felt that she would not be able to do so until she had delivered Violette's message and asked her doctor if he would write to the Secret Service in London and ask for the Bushells' address. The reply came back that she could not be given the address and that anyway she should not try to communicate with the family.

For years she tried to get any information that she could. She had a little restaurant on the quay at Morlaix where she lived and every time any British people came to eat there she would ask if they could help her. No one could. Her cousin lived in England and she tried to enlist his help, but, although he tried to find out where they were, he was unable to give her any information about the Bushell family either.

Then at Easter 1958 Marie decided that rather than have the priest visit her she would go to church. In her letter to Violette's parents she said:

> I prayed for Violette, our lost comrades. I had my eyes fixed on a tableau on the wall; suddenly I saw a vision of Violette on it, very plainly I saw her. I remain praying a little longer and went home. I sat down to have a cup of coffee but some unseen power was driving me on. I went to a cupboard and took out an old pocket wallet, mouldy with age. I did not know why, I had not touched it for over 12 years. I came back to the table and shook the contents on it; only an old bill, cheque book, two bits of paper folded up. The first one, a circular from the Red Cross, the other, a miracle had happened, it was a newspaper cutting, yellow, with our dear Violette's picture on it and Mr Bushell looking for his missing daughter. I could hardly believe it was true. When my daughter came in I ask, who put these papers in my wallet? She said it was her aunt in 1946 when I was so ill, but I never knew it. I had to do something this very day. I must write to my cousin again in England, tell him before I die I have to contact Violette's parents. He must ask his friend the journalist. The answer came two days later from the reporter Mr Bert Nash, he gave me your and Tania's address given to him by Mrs Cutbush of 3 Burnley Road.

I know you will be grieved to read all I have told you, but rest assure in knowing Violette was a noble girl, full of gaiety even in the terrible days she had to go through.

The letter did bring comfort to Mr and Mrs Bushell, in spite of the terrible details about Violette's captivity and when, later on, Marie Lecomte finally met members of the Bushell family she was, at last, able to kiss them for Violette as she had promised all those years before.

Tania grew up and finished her college course. She eventually decided to return to the land of her birth, where she now runs her own language school and translation service.

Dame Irene Ward MP had become very interested in the work of SOE following the publication of the book she wrote in 1955 about the FANY, called *F.A.N.Y. Invicta*. She made strenuous efforts to have Violette's George Cross changed to a Victoria Cross but to no avail. There was a curious amount of male opposition to the idea; there were even suggestions that the Victoria Cross was not an award that was open to women. This is not true, although to this day there are no female holders of the Victoria Cross.

In March 1964 a memorial plaque was dedicated to Violette and placed in the entrance to Lambeth Town Hall. It was the first of many memorials. The same year the Vincennes Estate was built in the borough of Lambeth and two of the buildings were named after the two female agents who had had a connection with the borough, Lilian Rolfe and Violette Szabo. The Greater London Council placed a blue plaque on the wall of the house at 18 Burnley Road, Stockwell, in 1981 and Stockwell Road School where Violette and her brothers were educated now has a memorial garden dedicated to the memory of Violette. There is a fuchsia in the garden which has been named after her. There are also other memorials at Beaulieu, site of the finishing schools, and at the cemetery at Brookwood in Surrey. Brookwood, when it was opened in 1854, was the largest cemetery in the world and was known as the London Necropolis. There are a number of military cemeteries within the grounds, covering an area of approximately thirty-seven acres, which are administered by the Commonwealth War Graves Commission and together form the largest military cemetery in the United Kingdom. The Brookwood Memorial, within the military section, commemorates 3500 dead of the Second World War who have no known graves, including Violette Szabo and her colleagues of SOE.

There were monuments and memorials in other countries too. Odette Hallowes donated a plaque, in memory of Violette Szabo, Lilian Rolfe, Denise Bloch and Cecily Lefort, which is on the memorial wall of the 'Grossbritannien' section at Ravensbrück concentration camp, now preserved as a museum. Mrs Hallowes unveiled the plaque at a ceremony on 10 June 1993, which was attended by former inmates of the camp, relatives and friends of the victims and members of SOE, the WAAF and the FANY. At the ceremony a message, sent by Her Majesty Queen Elizabeth the Queen Mother, was read out. It said:

> I am very pleased to learn of the ceremony to be held at Ravensbrück today to mark the sacrifice of four members of the Special Operations Executive (SOE) F Section who lost their lives in January and February 1945 and in remembrance of those who survived.
>
> The passage of time has not dulled the admiration which we who are left feel for those gallant members of a very wonderful force. Their memories will remain a shining example of courage and self-sacrifice which contributed in no small way to the outcome of World War II.

On 6 June 2000 Tania unveiled a memorial to her mother in Le Clos very close to where Violette and the other members of the Salesman 2 team had landed fifty-six years before.

Twenty years after the blue plaque had been put on the wall in Burnley Road a mural dedicated to Violette was unveiled on 26 June 2001. Tania Szabo was present at the ceremony and Virginia McKenna, who had played the part of her mother in the film, made a speech in which she said that although she did not look like Violette at all, she hoped that she had captured her spirit in her portrayal of her. A message from the veteran film director

Lewis Gilbert, who had worked on the film, was read out at the reception after the ceremony.

When I first met Tania in 1999 she told me that some people have questioned whether or not Violette should have left a baby to go to France and fight. This reaction puzzles Tania. As she pointed out, no one has questioned the fact that thousands of fathers, including her own, left their families to go off to war and never returned. Why should her mother be regarded any differently, simply because she was a woman?

The women of SOE were vital to the organization. They were much more able to melt into the background of occupied France than the men. Without their work the tasks of the men would have been made so much more difficult. Violette Szabo knew that her knowledge of France and her ability to speak the language were qualities that were in short supply. When her husband died she knew that she could not sit at home and let others take the responsibility for ensuring her family's freedom. She decided she had to take the responsibility herself and continue the fight for which her husband had given his life. Her ultimate sacrifice, and that of women like her, allowed other mothers to stay at home with their children and bring them up in peace.

Appendix A

SOE Charter

<u>MOST SECRET</u>
<u>WP (40)271</u>
<u>19th July 1940</u>

WAR CABINET
HOME DEFENCE (SECURITY) EXECUTIVE
SPECIAL OPERATIONS EXECUTIVE

Memorandum by the Lord President of the Council

1. The memorandum which I circulated to the Cabinet on 27th May (WP(40)172) gave particulars of the organisation of the Home Defence (Security) Executive, which was set up under the chairmanship of Lord Swinton to co-ordinate action against the Fifth Column.
2. In addition to presiding over the Home Defence (Security) Executive, Lord Swinton has been entrusted with the executive control of MI5 and is thus responsible for counter espionage activities in Great Britain.
3. The Prime Minister has now decided that Lord Swinton shall also exercise operational control over the work of MI6 in respect of all the activities of MI6 in Great Britain and in Eire. MI6 will also continue to place at the disposal of Lord Swinton all information in their posses-

sion which may have a bearing on Fifth Column activities in Great Britain or Eire.

4. The Prime Minister has further decided, after consultation with the Ministers concerned, that a new organisation shall be established forthwith to co-ordinate all action, by way of subversion and sabotage, against the enemy overseas. The Prime Minister requested me to set on foot this new organisation in consultation with those concerned. Action is accordingly being taken as follows:

   a. An organisation is being established to co-ordinate all action, by way of subversion and sabotage, against the enemy overseas. This organisation will be known as the Special Operations Executive.
   b. The Special Operations Executive will be under the chairmanship of Mr Dalton, the Minister of Economic Warfare.
   c. Mr Dalton will have the assistance of Sir Robert Vansittart.
   d. The Special Operations Executive will be provided with such additional staff as the Chairman and Sir Robert Vansittart may find necessary.
   e. The various departments and bodies taking part in underground activities will, for the time being, continue to be administered by the Ministers at present responsible for them.
   f. The departments and bodies affected which will now be co-ordinated by Mr Dalton are:

Title	Alternative Title	Administrative Authority
Sabotage Service	'D'	FO
MI(R)	-	WO
Department Electra House	Sir Campbell Stuart's Organization	Joint FO and Minister of Information

Mr Dalton will also have the co-operation of the Directors of Intelligence of the three Service Departments and of the Secret Intelligence Service (MI6) for the purpose of the work entrusted to him. Mr Dalton will also keep in touch with Lord Hankey

g. The Planning and direction of raids by formed bodies of British or Allied ships, troops or aircraft will remain the function of the Military authorities, but Mr Dalton will maintain touch with Departments planning such raids in order to afford any possible assistance through the channels he co-ordinates.
h. Any Department obtaining information likely to be of value to Mr Dalton will place their information at his disposal.
i. All operations of sabotage, secret subversive propaganda, the encouragement of civil resistance in occupied areas, the stirring up of insurrection, strikes, etc., in Germany or areas occupied by her will be submitted before being undertaken by any Department, to Mr Dalton for his approval.
j. Mr Dalton will co-ordinate the planning operations of underground warfare and will direct which organisation is to carry them out. He will be responsible for obtaining the agreement of the Secretary of State for Foreign Affairs or other Minister interested to any operation which is likely to affect their interests.
k. It will be important that the general plan for irregular offensive operations should be in step with the general strategical conduct of the war. With this end in view, Mr Dalton will consult the Chiefs of Staff as necessary, keeping them informed in general terms of his plans, and, in turn, receiving from them the broad strategical picture.

5. Lord Swinton and Mr Dalton will arrange for any consultation that may be mutually helpful or may be necessary to prevent overlapping between the Home Defence (Security) Executive and the Special Operations Executive. Normally, no doubt, consultation between their respective staffs will suffice for this purpose.

6. The Prime Minister has requested that Lord Swinton and Mr Dalton should regard me as the member of the War Cabinet whom they should consult and to whom any inter-Departmental difficulties should arise, would be referred.

(Int'd) N.C.

[Neville Chamberlain]

Privy Council Office, SW1
19th July 1940.

Appendix B

Medal citations
George Cross

Madame Szabo volunteered to undertake a particularly dangerous mission in France. She was parachuted into France in April 1944, and undertook the task with enthusiasm. In her execution of the delicate researches entailed she showed great presence of mind and astuteness. She was twice arrested by the German security authorities, but each time managed to get away. Eventually, however, with other members of her group, she was surrounded by the Gestapo in a house in the south-west of France. Resistance appeared hopeless, but Madame Szabo, seizing a Sten gun and as much ammunition as she could carry, barricaded herself in part of the house, and, exchanging shot for shot with the enemy, killed or wounded several of them. By constant movement she avoided being cornered and fought until she dropped exhausted. She was arrested and had to undergo solitary confinement. She was then continuously and atrociously tortured, but never by word or deed gave away any of her acquaintances, or told the enemy anything of value. She was ultimately executed. Madame Szabo gave a magnificent example of courage and steadfastness.

Croix de Guerre

REPUBLIQUE FRANÇAISE
CITATION

EXTRAIT DE L'ORDRE GENERAL No 3

Le Colonel RIVIER

Commandant la 5° Région des Forces Françaises
de l'Intérieur de la 12° Région Militaire

CITE A L'ORDRE DE LA DIVISION

Enseigne TAYLOR Vicky Alias SZABO Violette –
Corps Féminin F.A.N.Y

"Parachutée le 7 juin 1944 en France, stoppée au cours d'une mission de liaison le 10 juin à Salon-la-Tour (Corrèze) par un barrage allemand. A refuse de se render et s'est battue à l'aide de sa mitraillette pendant vingt minutes, tuant un caporal allemand. A dû se render faute de munitions. Emprisonnée à Limoges le 11 Juin, disparue le 12 Juin."

Ces citations comportent l'attribution de la Croix de Guerre 1939–1945 avec étoile d'argent.

Au Q.G., le 16 septembre 1944
Signé: RIVIER

(Parachuted into France on 7 June 1944, she was stopped by a German road block at Salon-la-Tour [Corrèze] on 10 June while undertaking a liaison mission. Refusing to give herself up she fought with her sub-machine gun for twenty minutes, killing a German corporal. She eventually had to give up for lack of ammunition. Imprisoned at Limoges on 11 June, she disappeared on 12 June.

This citation awards the Croix de Guerre 1939–45 with Silver Star.)

Appendix C

Awards for Salesman 1 and 2 circuits Citations for Decorations recommended by Philippe Liewer

Capt MORTIER.

Wounded twice by enemy fire, displayed the greatest gallantry in blowing up demolitions constantly for 8 days under enemy fire in the SUSSAC (Haute Vienne) area, in the second half of July 1944. Was wounded for the second time as he was endeavouring to make prisoners single-handed near MEZIERES (Indre) on the 4th September.

Hugues PACCAUD.

With the greatest coolness he managed to take his explosive charge into a heavily guarded ship-yard and blow up and sink an enemy minesweeper despite the presence of large number of German officials, and this only three hours before the ship was due to leave. At a later date he took part in a very successful attack on the transformer station at DIEPPEDALLE.

Lt.Col. GUINGOIN.

FFI chief Haute Vienne. During the heavy German attacks in the second half of July, 1944 in the SUSSAC area he was constantly heading counter-attacks and offensive patrols and ambushes. Mastered the situation in the most brilliant way, causing a known minimum of 320 casualties to the enemy for the loss of 31 of his men.

Capt. ROLET

Capitaine de Réserve, French Army, commanding the FFI Company known as Le Desert. With a total of 44 men he withstood, during three days on the 18th, 19th and 20th July 1944, in the forest of CHATEAUNEUF, the attacks of first 400 German infantrymen, reinforced at the end of the second day by 350 militia men, with no heavier armament than Bren Guns against heavy mortar fire and 37mm guns. Repulsed 6 different enemy companies, taking a very heavy toll of enemy casualties, and losing himself only one courrier. He allowed by this brilliant offensive action the major part of armament dumps to be evacuated to a quieter area, and prevented the occupation of SUSSAC, which would have meant at the time the complete dispersal of the Bistrot Maquis.

Appendix D

The Violette Szabo Museum

On 31 October 1998 an appeal was launched by Rosemary Rigby MBE, at the village hall in Much Dewchurch in Herefordshire. Rosemary is the owner of a house in the village of Wormelow called Cartref. It was formerly known as The Old Kennels and is the house in which Violette Szabo's aunt and uncle, Florence and Harry Lucas, once lived. It was here that Violette often visited and was where she rested between her two missions to France.

The aim of Rosemary Rigby's appeal was to start a collection in order to establish a museum in Violette's honour in the grounds of her home. Actress Virginia McKenna, who had played the part of Violette in the 1958 film *Carve Her Name with Pride*, supported the appeal.

The money began to arrive from people all over the world and the proposed museum was also allocated funds from the National Lottery. Rosemary Rigby has worked diligently and tirelessly to raise the funds that have enabled her to build the museum.

Eventually her dream was realized by the opening of the museum on 24 June 2000. The opening date was chosen as being the closest Saturday to what would have been Violette's seventy-ninth birthday. Hundreds of people arrived for the opening, including Tania Szabo, Bob Maloubier, Jean Claude Guiet, Leo Marks and Virginia McKenna, who performed the opening ceremony. A message from the then Speaker of the House of Commons, Betty Boothroyd, was read out.

Rosemary Rigby is determined to keep the memory of Violette Szabo alive. On the first anniversary of the opening she arranged a picnic in the grounds and hopes that this will become an annual event.

The museum is open to the public every Wednesday between April and October, but Rosemary will open it at other times by special request. She also welcomes groups of visitors, again by special arrangement.

Anyone wishing to visit the museum out of hours or to arrange a group visit should contact –

Rosemary Rigby
The Violette Szabo Museum
Cartref
Tump Lane
Wormelow
Herefordshire
HR2 8HN

Telephone 01981 540477

The museum can be found by taking the A49 from Hereford in the direction of Ross on Wye. The turning to Wormelow is alongside the Pilgrim Hotel at Much Birch, and Cartref is the first house on the left.

Appendix E

Executed women agents

Name	Circuit	Fate
Yolande Beekman (*Yvonne*)	Musician	Executed Dachau, September 1944
Denise Bloch (*Ambroise*)	Clergyman	Executed Ravensbrück, January 1945
Andrée Borrrel (*Denise*)	Physician	Executed Natzweiler, July 1944
Madeleine Damerment (*Solange*)	Bricklayer	Executed Dachau, September 1944
Noor Inayat Khan (*Madeleine*)	Cinema-Phono	Executed Dachau, September 1944
Cecily Lefort (*Alice*)	Jockey	Executed Ravensbrück, early 1945
Vera Leigh (*Simone*)	Inventor	Executed Natzweiler, July 1944

Sonia Olschanezky (*unknown*)	Juggler	Executed Natzweiler, July 1944
Eliane Plewman (*Gaby*)	Monk	Executed Dachau, September 1944
Lilian Rolfe (*Nadine*)	Historian	Executed Ravensbrück, January 1945
Diana Rowden (*Paulette*)	Acrobat/ Stockbroker	Executed Natzweiler, July 1944
Yvonne Rudellat (*Jacqueline*)	Physician	Died in Belsen, April 1945 following ill treatment.
Violette Szabo (*Louise*)	Salesman	Executed Ravensbrück, January 1945

Appendix F

. . . and finally . . .

While undertaking the research for this book I came across many stories which surprised me. Many of the long-held 'truths' about Violette Szabo proved not to be true at all. I hope that in these cases I have been able to set the record straight.

Trying to separate the fact from the fiction has not always been easy, which is why the following appears here rather than in the main part of the book. I have not been able to either prove or disprove what follows and I leave it to the reader to decide for him or her self.

Shortly before I was due to deliver the manuscript of this book to my publisher I received some startling information from a hitherto impeccable source. I was told that Leo Marks had not written Violette Szabo's code poem, *The Life That I Have*. My source told me that it had, in fact, been the work of John Pudney, who has many other poems to his credit, including the well-known wartime poem *For Johnny*. The story was that Mr Pudney, who was himself a publisher, had been approached by a film company in 1958 and asked to write a poem, which would be used in a film about SOE to be made that year. So far as I have been able to check, *Carve Her Name With Pride* was the only such film made that year. I am not an expert in poetry, but I have been told that the form of *The Life That I Have* is consistent with some of the other poems written by Mr Pudney.

My first reaction was disbelief. The film *Carve Her Name With Pride* had, after all, been made from the book of the same name, which was written in 1956, two years before John Pudney was said to have been asked to write the poem. However, when I checked back with the book I found that the poem is not mentioned. Indeed there is no mention at all of a code poem.

As early as 1942 Leo Marks himself had highlighted the flaws in using a poem which might be recognized by German interrogators or could possibly be obtained from the agent by torture. His solution to the problem was to use a worked-out key or WOK on a letter one-time pad that was printed on silk and could be cut away and destroyed after use. Apparently once this system was officially adopted the poem code was only used as a back up. It is true that Marks wrote many of the poems that were used, but his poetry, as quoted in his book *Between Silk and Cyanide*, would appear to be amusing doggerel rather than love poetry.

I understand that there is no record on her file of which poem Violette would have used, had the need arisen, but Leo Marks had claimed in his book that:

> A film was made about Violette Szabo called *Carve Her Name With Pride*, and I allowed its producer, Daniel Angel, to use the poem in his film providing that its author's name wasn't disclosed.

Odette Hallowes acted as an advisor on the film and it was she, presumably, who told Daniel Angel about the poem code. However, in view of the many inaccuracies in the film it would be surprising if he went to the trouble of finding out the exact poem that had been allocated to Violette. In the film the poem is attributed to Etienne, who could not speak English and would, therefore, never have been able to write it. However, it is a love poem and attributing it to her husband would make sense for the film.

It has also been pointed out that SOE files were still closed to the public in 1958 (some files remain closed in 2001) and one wonders whether or not it would have been possible for Daniel Angel to use the exact poem, whatever it may have been, because of the problems associated with closed documents. From that point of view alone it may have made sense to commission a poem for the film.

Whenever the poem is quoted in written form, it is invariably followed by '© Leo Marks'. I contacted the Patent Office to double-check the regulations regarding copyright and was told, as I suspected, that there is no set procedure for claiming copyright. An author merely has to assert his or her right to claim and it is done. There is no registration of the claim.

John Pudney died in 1977. It occurred to me that if he had been asked to write a poem for the film this request might have been put in writing. I discovered that, although he was British, his papers are now held at the University of Texas in Austin. Tara Wenger, a very helpful research librarian at the University, made a search of his papers for me, but was unable to find anything that would settle the matter one way or the other and so it looks as if this particular part of the puzzle may remain a mystery for ever.

Bibliography

Bidwell, Shelford, *The Women's Royal Army Corps*, Leo Cooper Limited, 1977

Brew Kerr, Dorothy, *The Girls Behind the Guns, with the ATS in World War II*, Robert Hale, 1990

Buckmaster, Maurice, *Specially Employed, The Story of British Aid to French Patriots of the Resistance*, The Batchworth Press, 1952

They Fought Alone, Odhams Press Limited, 1958

Butler, Ewan, *Amateur Agent*, George G. Harrap & Co Limited, 1963

Chapman, Roger, *A record of the history & inhabitants of Hampstead Norreys Parish – Village properties & families, 1700–1990*

Clark, Freddie, *Agents by Moonlight*, Tempus Publishing Limited, 1999

Cookridge, E.H., *Inside SOE*, Arthur Barker Limited, 1966

Cunningham, Cyril, *Beaulieu: The Finishing School for Secret Agents*, Leo Cooper Limited, 1998

Churchill, Winston S., *The Second World War*, Cassell & Company Limited, 1964

Dady, Margaret, *A Woman's War; Life in the ATS*, The Book Guild Limited, 1986

Dear, Ian, *Sabotage & Subversion: Stories from the files of the SOE and OSS*, Arms & Armour, 1996

de Gaulle Anthonioz, Geneviève, *God Remained Outside, an Echo of Ravensbrück*, Souvenir Press, 2000

Dufurnier, Denise, *Ravensbrück, The Women's Camp of Death*, George Allen & Unwin, 1948
Escott, Squadron Leader Beryl E., *Mission Improbable*, Patrick Stephens Limited, 1991
Foot, M.R.D., *SOE in France*, HMSO, 1966
Höhne, Heinz, *The Order of the Death's Head: The story of Hitler's SS*, Pan Books, 1972
Jackson, Robert, *The Secret Squadrons*, Robson Books, 1983
Jones, Liane, *A Quiet Courage*, Bantam Press, 1990
Kedward, H.R., *Occupied France, Collaboration and Resistance 1940–1944*, Blackwell Publishers, 1985
Mackenzie, William, *The Secret History of SOE, the Special Operations Executive 1940–1945*, St Ermin's Press, 2000
Marshall, Bruce, *The White Rabbit*, Evans Brothers Limited, 1952
Mason, T.J., *Violette Szabo GC, a very special lady*, T.J. Mason, 1995
Minney, R.J., *Carve her Name with Pride*, George Newnes Limited, 1956
Nockolds, Harold, *Lucas, The first 100 years*, David & Charles, 1976
Overton Fuller, Jean, *The German Penetration of SOE, France 1941–1944*, George Mann Books, 1996
Parker, John, *Inside the Foreign Legion*, Piatkus, 1998
Schoenbrun, David, *Maquis, Soldiers of the Night: The Story of the French Resistance*, Robert Hale, 1981
Shirer, William L., *The Rise and Fall of the Third Reich, A History of Nazi Germany*, Pan Books, 1964
Snyder, Louis L., *Encyclopedia of the Third Reich*, Wordsworth Editions Limited, 1998
Sweet-Escott, Bickham, *Baker Street Irregular*, Methuen & Co Limited, 1965
Tickell, Jerrard, *Odette, The Story of a British Agent*, Pan Books Limited, 1965
Tillion, Germaine, *Ravensbrück: an eyewitness account of a women's concentration camp*, Anchor Books, 1975
Tomlinson, Steve, *Violette Szabo*, The Violette Szabo GC Museum, 2001
Travers, Susan, *Tomorrow to be Brave*, Bantam Press, 2000

Verity, Hugh, *We Landed by Moonlight*, AirData Publications Limited, 1995
Vickers, Philip, *DAS REICH, 2nd SS Panzer Division, Das Reich – Drive to Normandy*, Leo Cooper Limited, 2000
Ward DBE, MP, Irene, *F.A.N.Y. Invicta*, Hutchinson, 1955
West, Nigel, *Secret War, The story of SOE, Britain's Wartime Sabotage Organisation*, Hodder & Stoughton, 1992
Windrow, Martin, *French Foreign Legion 1914–1945*, Osprey Publishing, 1999
Wright, Michael, ed. *The World at Arms*, The Reader's Digest Association Limited, 1989

Index